MILITARY MEMOIRS

Edited by
Brigadier Peter Young
D.S.O., M.C., M.A., F.S.A., F.R.HIST.S.

A non-commissioned officer in the uniform of the 73rd Regiment of
Infantry during the occupation of Paris, 1815

MILITARY MEMOIRS

Thomas Morris

The Napoleonic Wars

Edited by

JOHN SELBY

ARCHON BOOKS
1968

© Longmans, Green and Co Ltd 1967
First published 1967

This edition first published in the
United States of America by Archon Books, 1968,
Hamden, Connecticut

Printed in Great Britain by
W. & J. Mackay & Co Ltd, Chatham, Kent

SBN: 208 00631 1

Contents

General Introduction
to the Series

by PETER YOUNG

Dr Johnson: *Every man thinks meanly of himself for not having been a soldier, or not having been at sea.*
Boswell: *Lord Mansfield does not.*
Dr Johnson: *Sir, if Lord Mansfield were in a company of admirals and generals who'd seen service he'd wish to creep under the table.*

None can doubt that Samuel Johnson, so formidable with tongue and pen, was also stout of heart. Yet it would be wrong to suppose that these remarks on military service were not inspired by a genuine sentiment. One suspects that he was a bit of a fire-eater at heart. For all his wisdom he could envy the exploits of less learned contemporaries who faced powder and shot. It is an attitude that endures even as late as the last half of the twentieth century.

It is the common lot of fighting men that they have little to show for their efforts. Their satisfaction seldom comes in the shape of material rewards, unless they are at the very top of their profession. They must be content with the private feeling that they have played their part. It may be no more complicated than the atavistic instinct to strike a blow for hearth and home, the grim satisfaction of the Gallic warrior who had killed a Roman.

But nowadays it is not given to everyone to be a soldier, or to serve in the air or on the seas. One earns no great reputation as a seer by predicting that the memoirs of those who serve in World War III will be somewhat brief, or that the struggle itself will be nasty. If people are still interested in wars, it may be better for them to satisfy their curiosity by pondering those of the past rather than provoking those of the future.

In planning a series of this sort there are a bewildering variety of factors to be considered. Of these perhaps the chief to be taken into account is the fundamental question: 'Why do people read Military History?' Is it because truth is more attractive than fiction? Baron de Marbot, although his tales had unquestionably improved in the telling, has an interest which Brigadier Gerard, despite the narrative skill of Conan Doyle, cannot rival. Marbot's memory could play him false in matters of detail, but not as to the sense of period. He brings to life the atmosphere of the Grand Army in which he served. Marbot, regrettably, is too well known, both in French and English, to parade with the veterans of this series. We have endeavoured to present memoirists who for one reason or another are relatively unknown to the English-speaking public.

In modern times memoir-writing seems to have become the prerogative of generals. One is not, however, without hopes of finding a voice or two from the ranks to conjure up the fields of Flanders or the deserts of North Africa. Of course, we have not rejected generals altogether. But on the whole we have tried to rescue 'old swordsmen' from oblivion rather than, say, a religious enthusiast, like Colonel Blackader—more concerned with the salvation of his soul than the deployment of his battalion. The fighting soldier is more attractive than an officer with a distinguished series of staff appointments to his credit; the tented field has an appeal which the dull round of garrison life cannot rival.

If such knowing officers as Captains Kincaid and Mercer or Monsieur de la Colonie, or such hard-bitten foot soldiers as Rifleman Harris or Sergeant Wheeler do not appear here, it is only because their excellent narratives are comparatively well known and easy of access.

We have avoided those veterans who, their Napier at their elbow, submerge their personal recollections in a mass of ill-digested second-hand campaign history. These are the most maddening of all. What details they could have given us had they chosen to! One reads that Colonel So-and-so dined with General Such-and-such. But why can't the fellow go on to tell us whether the general kept a good table, or what sort of conversationalist he was? Was he liked by his men? There is all the difference in the world between Rifleman Harris, who gives us such a wonderful picture of General Robert Crauford on the retreat to Corunna, and Captain William Bragge, who fought at Salamanca and whose Journal tells us exactly nothing about it!

The trouble is that memoirists take so much for granted. They assume that we know all about the military organization and tactics of their day. And so we must just be thankful for small mercies. You will not get a fight on every page, but gradually a picture is built up. One comes to visualize the manners of a bygone age, to see how people then could endure the privations of a campaign, the rough surgery of the battlefield, or the administrative neglect of their commanders. In the end we come almost to speak their language, and to hear them speak.

When they are promoted or rewarded we can share their pleasure. *'C'était un des plus beaux jours de ma vie!'* Marbot naïvely remarks when recounting the successes of his younger days, and we are almost as pleased as he.

But if you prefer to read these adventures rather than to emulate them, that, too, is understandable.

'How sweet the music of a *distant* drum.'

Introduction

Thomas Morris joined the Loyal Volunteers of St George's, Middlesex, in 1812, when he was sixteen. He seems to have had a genuine desire to become a regular soldier; and when his brother joined the 73rd Regiment in the Tower, having often visited the regiment, he soon wanted to join it.

When the 73rd moved to Harwich for embarkation to the Continent, Morris tried to enlist with them. After some difficulty he eventually succeeded in doing so, and thus sailed to the Baltic. The force landed on the island of Rügen, and took part in a little known operation in the north of Germany, which included the Battle of Göhrde. The army to which Morris was attached was composed of Hanoverians, Swedes, Russians, and the 73rd Regiment and half a rocket-battery of artillery from Britain.

Morris's next campaign was in Holland in 1813–14. Here he served under Lieutenant-General Sir Thomas Graham of Barrosa fame. Finally Morris was present with his regiment at Waterloo in 1815, and took part in the occupation of Paris afterwards.

After the war he returned home to England, going first to Nottingham, and then to Wolverhampton and Birmingham.

In his last chapter he describes the reduction of the short-lived 2nd Battalion of the 73rd Regiment at Chelmsford, when the men who were left were posted to the 1st Battalion in Ceylon. He is obviously sentimental about his soldiering, and fond of his regiment, for, when the major formed them up for the breaking up of his battalion, and made a very impressive speech, he records that 'there was scarcely a man among us who did not shed a tear'.

When Morris had completed his seven years, he was particularly urged by the officer in command to extend his time and join the 1st Battalion in Ceylon; but he decided to take his discharge. He then returned to London where he had been born and bred, and, according to himself, 'attained a respectable position in civil society'.

Rifleman Harris in his Recollections gives the impression of admiring his officers too much for it to be genuine. Private Wheeler writes well and creates both atmosphere and interest; but Captain Liddell Hart has to do a lot of editing to make him coherent. Costello, according to a contemporary reviewer, gives a true and vivid picture of a soldier's life. Morris has a jealous streak it is true, recording: 'In the various histories which have been published, the greatest praise has invariably been given to those regiments whose officers were of high birth and aristocratic connexions; while other corps, not possessing these fortuitous advantages, have had the mortification to find their services pass altogether unnoticed'; and he gives this as the reason for writing his book. In spite of this, however, in my opinion Morris is the best of this group. He is a born storyteller, and the description of his soldiering over these three years is quite fascinating. The first edition of 1845, published by James Madden and Co., was spoilt by the inclusion of several descriptive passages culled from the history books of his day. These are unfortunate, as are some of the poems he saw fit to include; I have been quite ruthless in striking them out. In their place I have brought in three descriptions of my own of the three campaigns in which Sergeant Morris and the 73rd took part, and three maps attempting to include most of the places named by Sergeant Morris in the text of his book.

Morris's spelling is generally good and has needed little correction except in the case of a few place names where a more usual form has sometimes been given in brackets on the first mention of the place. Morris was a Cockney (see p.37), alert and with a good memory. He seldom names his old officers incorrectly and accurately recalls the actual dates of the moves of his battalion. His descriptions fit in well with the other scanty records of some of the engagements he covers, as well as with the better known ones like Waterloo.

As appendices I have made free use of Cannon's history of the 2nd Battalion of the 73rd which was disbanded in 1817 but may be said, with the whole of the 73rd, to live on as one of the regiments which went to form the Black Watch.

Also included is a biography, from Cannon's history, of the second Lord Harris who commanded the 73rd during the service of Sergeant Morris, and a description of the regiment from *Goddard and Booth's Military Costumes of Europe, 1812.*

The information in my footnotes concerning the officers of the 73rd Regiment is taken from *The Waterloo Roll Call.*

I would like to thank the staff of the National Army Museum and in particular, Mr W. Y. Carman, Acting Director, for the great help they gave me during the editing of this book.　　　　JOHN SELBY

Preface

In the various histories which have been published, recording the events of the late war, the greatest praise has invariably been given to those regiments whose officers were of high birth and aristocratic connexions; while other corps, not possessing these fortuitous advantages, have had the mortification to find their services pass altogether unnoticed. This cannot be imputed to fault in the historian, as he derived his information from the official dispatches; the onus, then, must rest with the General commanding; and, without imputing to him any corrupt motive, we may state it to have been but natural for him to make the most honourable mention of those regiments, whose officers he was desirous of recommending to the special notice of headquarters. However, favouritism always has existed, and doubtless always will. I shall endeavour, therefore, in the following pages, simply to place on record some of the exploits of the regiment in which I served, as well as of some others with whom we occasionally co-operated; but who, like ourselves, had not the honour to be noticed in dispatches, for the reasons I have before stated.

As I have no written data to go on, but trust entirely to memory, if any inaccuracies shall be detected, I hope it will be imputed to that circumstance, rather than to any wilful intention on my part, to record events which I do not know or believe to be true.

T.M.

Recollections

I

The meanest soldier, fired by glory's rage,
Believes his name enroll'd in history's page;
O! dear deceit—the statesman's firmest friend,
By which the rabble crowd promote their end.

In the year 1812, though then only sixteen, I had the honour to belong
to the Loyal Volunteers of St George's, Middlesex. The object of
most of my comrades, in joining that gallant corps, was to avail
themselves of the exemption thereby secured to them—from being
compelled to serve in the Militia. Such, however, was not my motive
in joining them, as I was not old enough to have any fear about being
drawn. But various were the stratagems practised by persons to escape
serving. One young man I knew well, who was just married, when
he received a summons to attend at the Court-house in Wellclose
Square, to show cause, if he had any, why he should not be sworn
in; and, as he had very considerable objections to serving His Majesty
in the Tower Hamlets' Militia, he hit upon the following expedient
to avoid it. He went home, and feigned to be extremely ill; sent for
the doctor, and made a variety of complaints; took all the physic
that was sent him, laid in bed, and let his beard grow until the time
came for his appearance, when, borrowing a pair of crutches, he
hobbled along to the Court-house; and on presenting himself before
the magistrate, his reply to the usual question, as to what objection he
had to serve, was, that he had been very ill, and was very poor, but
if they would give him a ticket for the hospital, as soon as he was
recovered he would be at their service. The fellow's appearance was
altogether so emaciated and miserable, that the worthy and sagacious
functionary at once declared him unfit to serve, and desired him to go
about his business. The circumstance became known to the shopmates
of the man, who frequently indulged in a laugh at the expense of the
magistrate; however, the man saved something like ten pounds by the
manoeuvre, as it would have taken that at least to provide a substitute.

As much as sixty pounds has been paid for a substitute in the militia, in war time; and, as I have before observed, to avoid those charges was the principal inducement to many persons in becoming volunteers; but other motives influenced me. I was particularly fond of reading the heart-stirring accounts of sieges and battles; and the glorious achievements of the British troops in Spain, following each other in rapid succession, created in me an irrepressible desire for military service; so, as the first step towards it, I became a Volunteer, and, oh! how proud did I feel when having gone through my course of drill, I was permitted to join the ranks. Even now I often think of the delightful sensation I experienced on our forming on the regimental parade-ground, and marching from thence to the Tenter-ground, in Goodman's Fields—at that time a most convenient place for the exercise of troops, and where our evolutions and martial exercises excited the admiration and wonder of crowds of nursery-maids and children, who invariably attended on such occasions. Then, how delightful on our return home, to parade the streets in our splendid uniform, exhibiting ourselves as the brave defenders of our country, should the Corsican attempt to carry into effect his threatened invasion of England.

Never shall I forget the occasion, when we were ordered to proceed to the Forest, for the display of a grand sham fight between us and the Ratcliff Volunteers! The ground selected for the event, was where Fairlop Fair is held, and on the day appointed, we left town at six a.m., in the midst of the greatest excitement, accompanied by a great number of our friends as also by sundry wagons, for the conveyance of the sick or wounded, together with some covered carts and a brewer's dray, containing abundance of ham, beef, and bread, as well as a plentiful supply of ale and porter, which good things, it was understood, were for distribution among us, if we should perform our duty manfully in the encounter. How exhilarating, on our road to the scene of action, to be saluted by the cheers of the crowd, the waving of handkerchiefs, the shouting of boys, the thrilling tones of the bugle, and the merry fife and drum. On our arrival at the ground, we found our antagonists had already taken up their position. We were allowed some half-hour's breathing-time, during which, the band of the Tower Hamlets' Militia—whose services had been specially retained—enlivened us by the performance of some martial airs, calculated to inflame our minds with that enthusiasm so necessary to constitute the character of the soldier.

At length the time for action arrived. We fell in and commenced the duties of the day; which consisted in marching and counter-marching, attacking and retreating, forming squares to repulse imaginary attacks of cavalry, and firing some thirty pounds of blank cartridges at each other. At last, the moment came which was to close our operations by a grand charge with fixed bayonets. The two regiments faced each other in line, and after each firing a volley, the men being directed to fire low, that their shots might be more effectual, the lines advanced, the word 'Charge!' was given, 'Forward, forward!' and on we went with the desperate determination of men resolved to conquer or die. When we had arrived within about twenty paces of each other, our commanding officers, fully satisfied of our coolness, and bravery, and unwilling to expose us to unnecessary danger, gave the word 'Halt!' and thereby relieved the apprehension of those who thought a collision unavoidable, and who much admired the ability of our officers in preventing danger so suddenly by giving the word 'halt'. Not being able to recollect that little word, led a colonel of the Warwickshire Militia into an awkward predicament. He was very unpopular with his men; and was one day exercising them in a field that was bounded by a deep ditch of black muddy water. Occasionally, when excited, the colonel had an impediment in his speech, which unfortunately affected him at this time, when by his own order, the regiment was charging in line. He was on horseback, retiring as they advanced, and for the life of him he could not think of or ejaculate the word 'Halt!' The men continued to advance, and the unfortunate commander still retiring from the bayonet's point, was at length driven with his horse into the black ditch.

But to return from this digression. Having performed our evolution to the satisfaction of our commanding officer, we were permitted to retire beneath the ample foliage of the Forest trees, there to enjoy ourselves with the good things provided for us; and there being no restriction in the serving out as to quantity, we were able to invite those of our friends, who had accompanied us from town: and after doing ample justice to the stock of provisions, we formed into parties, and indulged in the merry song and dance. When it was thought we had sufficiently enjoyed ourselves, we were ordered to prepare for the march home; but whether it was the effects of the weather, or the potency of the ale and porter, truth compels me to admit, that our return was not of the orderly, soldier-like description of our journey outwards in the morning; and many of the men were compelled to avail themselves of the conveyance of the wagons. However, we returned in safety, deposited our colours at the major's residence, and retired to our respective homes; much satisfied with our trip. Very often since that time, (when I have been exposed to the realities of a soldier's life, its dangers, its fatigues, its privations) have I thought of our Forest mimic fight, and wished that we could, on all occasions, have the same liberal provision made for our wants.

About the time I have been speaking of, there lay in the Tower, the second battalion of the 73rd Regiment (Highlanders). They bore on their colours and accoutrements the word 'Mangalore', from the fact of the first battalion having been engaged at the storming of the fortress of that name in the East Indies: and it so happened, that my brother, who had been in the Staffordshire Militia, volunteered into this regiment. Probably his principal reason was, that on joining them in the Tower, he would, for a time, be near home, and, from this circumstance, I contracted a sort of intimacy with the 73rd, and felt at times almost ashamed of being only half a soldier.

73rd Regiment of Foot

This Regiment was originally the 2nd Battalion of the 42nd, or Royal Highlanders, and was raised in the American War. At the peace in 1783, it obtained its present number on the disbanding of the old 73rd: from that period until 1806, it was stationed in the East Indies, and, for its excellent behaviour at the Siege of Mangalore, obtained the honour of bearing the name of that place on its colours and appointments; it was also at the siege of Seringapatam in 1799. After the siege it was employed on very active service under Sir Arthur Wellesley, until its Embarkation; and on its return to England it was quartered at Greenwich, and subsequently in Scotland, for the purpose of recruiting, being at the time a Highland Regiment; on being completed to its Establishment, it was ordered to New South Wales, to relieve the 102nd Regiment, and it is at present stationed there under Lieut.- General Macquarrie acting Governor.

'The 2nd Battalion of this Regiment was formed in 1809; it was always a very favorite Regiment, and was soon completed by Volunteers from the Militia; it has not been as yet on service, and is now doing Duty at the Tower of London, commanded by Lieutenant-Colonel Harris.

'The facings of this Regiment are green; the Privates have crooked Lace, similar to the 1st Guards; and its Appointments are equal, if not superior, to any Regiment in His Majesty's Service.'

'Motto "Mangalore".'[1]

1 From Goddard and Booth, *Military Costumes of Europe.*

My ardour for military life was somewhat damped, by the cruelty practised on a number of invalids, from various regiments then serving in Spain, many of them suffering from recent wounds, and all of them, more or less, affected by the severity of the duties they had been subjected to. They were under the command of an officer who exacted from them the strictest attention to their duty, and punished the slightest breach thereof with two or three hundred lashes. Often has my heart bled to see those poor fellows incapacitated—by wounds or disease—from further active service, returned to their native land, for which they had been shedding their blood, and, instead of receiving that commiseration to which they were entitled, to see such men tied to the halberts and their backs lacerated, for the most trifling fault, was really horrible:—not only disgraceful to the monster who ordered and superintended them, but reflecting also indelible infamy on the government which could tolerate them. The frequency and gross inhumanity of those punishments at length, called forth indignant remonstrances from the public, through the press; which led to the removal of the Colonel and the pensioning off the unfortunate invalids. Having witnessed many of those punishments, I felt somewhat less disposed to hazard life and limb, in a service, with the probability of being repaid with such gross inhumanity and ingratitude.

The 73rd were not, however, suffered to remain long in the Tower. They received the route for Colchester in the first instance, from whence they were expected to proceed to Harwich for embarkation. I accompanied my brother as far as Chelmsford; it was my desire to join them, but he refused to allow me, and I reluctantly returned to town. In a few days, I received a letter, informing me, they were on board at Harwich, and only waiting for a fair wind: their destination was not known.

While brooding over my disappointment in not being allowed to go with them, I most accidentally met with an old comrade of my brother, who had volunteered with him into the 73rd, and had been on furlough to see his friends. I expressed to him my desire to go, and finding his efforts to dissuade me unavailing, he agreed to meet me at six o'clock next morning. After a restless night, produced by the anxiety and distress which I knew my sudden departure would cause to my parents, I left about four o'clock in the morning, without taking leave of a single individual so fearful was I of being again disappointed. I left a note for my parents, praying their forgiveness and hoping all would end well. At six, I met my fellow traveller, at the Black Swan, at Bow, and after taking some refreshment we proceeded on our journey, amidst the merry ringing of the church bells, being the 29th of May, the anniversary of King Charles's Restoration [*in 1660*].

My comrade, whose name was Moore, was under the necessity of reaching Colchester that night, his time having expired, and owing to the bustle of so many troops embarking at Harwich, the coaches were all overloaded, so that the only chance we had of riding was by the return post-chaises. Being fortunate enough to get two or three lifts with these, we contrived to walk the rest of the distance. My companion was a good-humoured, pleasant fellow, full of anecdote; and amused me on the road by relating the various plans adopted in militia regiments to induce men to volunteer into regiments of the line. The militia would be drawn up in line, and the officers, or noncommissioned officers, from the regiments requiring volunteers, would give a glowing description of their several regiments, describing the victories they had gained and the honours they had acquired, and conclude by offering, as a bounty, to volunteers for life £14; to volunteers for the limited period of seven years, £11. If these inducements were not effectual in getting men, then coercive measures were adopted; heavy and long drills, and field exercises were forced on them; which were so oppressive, that to escape them, the men would embrace the alternative and join the regulars.

It was late in the evening when we reached Colchester, having walked thirty miles and ridden twenty-two; we went direct to the barracks, where my companion was at once admitted, and reported himself to his officer. It being after hours, they would not let him out again that night, nor would they let me in; so that, tired as I was, I was compelled to go in search of a lodging—rather a difficult thing to get, as the town was so full of troops. I was at length accommodated at a low public-house, called the 'Harrow', near the barracks, and being much fatigued with our long walk, I went to the bed allotted me in the attic, extending the whole breadth of the house, and containing some twelve beds of the most miserable description (as I then thought). However, as I was too tired to seek better accommodation, and as I was about entering on a situation in life which would necessarily subject me to many privations, I made up my mind to take life as it should come, and to do my best to struggle through its disagreeables; but I must confess, that on contrasting the wretched accommodation I now had, with the clean and comfortable home I had just left, I began seriously to reflect whether I had not better retrace my steps, as I still had the power to do so.

While discussing this subject with myself, I fell asleep, and had a strange medley of dreams, which rendered my repose anything but refreshing.

Having had my breakfast, and paid my reckoning, I wended my way towards the barracks, still thinking, at times, that I had better go back; however, on I went—found out the room where Moore was lodged, and went with him to Major [*Dawson*] Kelly, commanding the depot, who seemed pleased with my appearance, and sent me with a note to the surgeon of the 4th, or King's Own Regiment of Foot, then lying in the same barracks. That regiment was then on parade, and it was a punishment-parade—some sixteen poor fellows were waiting to receive their allowances, varying from 200 to 500 lashes: while this was going on I had no opportunity of seeing the surgeon, whose presence in the square was necessary during the punishment.

A gentleman standing near me, inquired of another the name or number of the regiment, and the answer he received was, that the men were called the King's Own, but he thought the officers must be the Devil's Own. This circumstance had almost overcome my desire for glory; and I was leaving the place to return home, when I met the major, to whom I related the reason I had not delivered his note, and he then sent me with a sergeant to another doctor, by whom I was examined and pronounced fit for service. The same sergeant then went with me to the town-hall, to witness my attestation before the magistrate. Before going in, however, we thought it desirable to obtain some refreshment, and having ordered a steak for two, while it was getting ready, the sergeant, a very intelligent Scotchman, gave me some good advice; and on learning that I was only seventeen, he told me to make it eighteen, as all under that age was boys' service, and reckoned nothing, either for extra pay or pension.

Having dispatched the steak, with sundry glasses of ale, we proceeded to the magistrate's office, and went through the customary form of attestation being sworn in to serve His Majesty, King George the Third, for the space of seven years. They sadly wanted me to enlist for life, but I thought seven years quite long enough for a trial. I felt somewhat more satisfied now that the deed was done: there was no longer any 'halting between two opinions'. I had no longer the power to go back.

On my return to the barracks, I immediately obtained a suit of regimentals and throwing aside my civilian's dress, I was that evening parading the town *à la militaire*; and no one who saw me would have supposed I had only been enlisted that day.

Next morning, at my own request, I was sent to drill; and while so occupied, I observed the major paying great attention to my movements: and calling me to him, and addressing me rather sternly, he said, 'Young man, you have been in the service before.' I assured him I had not been in any other than a corps of Volunteers. 'Well', said he, his face brightening up a little, 'if that is the case, the proficiency you have acquired in your exercise is highly creditable to you; if the volunteers were all as perfect, they would not be so much ridiculed as they are.'

Taking advantage of the major's good feeling towards me, I requested as a favour, that he would allow me to join the regiment which was still detained at Harwich by contrary winds, as he was going with a draft of 150 men in a few days. He expressed his regret that it was not in his power to grant my request, as the men were already selected, and their names forwarded to the Horse Guards, but he said he would take care I should come out with the next draft.

I then begged permission to visit my brother, at Harwich, which he readily complied with, and I had a pass for three days. So drawing a portion of my bounty, I started off immediately; and on my arrival at Harwich, hired a boat, and boarded the headquarter's ship, the *Old Saragossa*. The men all crowded round me, to learn the news from the depot. I reported myself to the colonel, and obtained leave for my brother to go on shore with me. We did not go directly, as it was near the time of serving out the grog, and some of them insisted I should take a can with them. I also partook of some beef and pudding, part of that day's allowance, after which, we went on shore, and spent the rest of the day and night at the 'Old Fishing Smack'.

Next morning, as we were strolling through the town, we met the colonel [*William George Harris*] who, till the time for sailing should arrive, was lodging with his family, at the 'Three Cups'. As I had still a strong desire to go with the regiment, I made the request, with which he seemed pleased. He asked when my pass expired? I told

1 See Appendix II for his biography.

him that I was to return to Colchester next day. 'Well,' said he, 'go back tomorrow, and I'll see what can be done.' I thanked him for his kindness, and we spent the rest of the day on board.

Next morning, I started early for Colchester; but whether it was the heat of the sun, or the indulgences of the last two days, I was so completely exhausted that I sought a shady spot and had a comfortable sleep on the grass for a couple of hours, when I was roused by a gentleman travelling in a chaise, who inquired the direction in which I was journeying, and on my naming Colchester he invited me to join him, which of course I did with great pleasure, being very glad of the opportunity; as I should otherwise have had to walk the whole distance. I found the gentleman a very pleasing companion, as well as a liberal one, for he stood paymaster for the refreshment we had on the road.

Having a good horse, we were not long reaching Colchester; and on getting out of the chaise, I expressed my thanks for his kindness; but he cut me short, by observing, 'that it was to serve himself he had done it. The fact is,' said he, 'that I have a great deal of money about me; and the roads about here are hardly safe just now, as there are so many old smugglers, and one rogue or another about, and I thought I might as well have a guard: so, my good fellow, I wish you good-bye, and God bless you!' then giving his horse a slight touch with the whip, he was out of sight in an instant.

They were much surprised, at the barracks, at my early return, not expecting me before night. I reported myself to the major [Kelly], and he informed me that he had received instruction from the colonel to include me in the detachment, which was to go on the third day from that time.

We were now all bustle and excitement; some of the men was not at all desirous of going, but I felt as much joy as if I had been going a journey of pleasure.

The morning of our departure came, and I received the rest of my bounty, with the exception of about two pounds, which I was told would be paid me on my arrival at Harwich. The distance from Colchester was twenty miles, which we had to accomplish in one day; a tolerably long day's march for young soldiers. We did not reach our destination until late in the afternoon, and immediately embarked on board a small brig, of about 200 tons, called the *Gratitude*. We were much crowded, and the prospect of going a voyage, in so small a vessel, was not very pleasant. On the colonel coming on board, I requested permission to sail in the *Saragossa*, along with my brother; he promised to consider of it, and, in the course of the day, my request led to an enquiry, as to whether the whole of us could not be transferred there. The result was, that we were all removed immediately, and the brig we had left was to accompany us filled with stores, which she was previously intended for.

The *Saragossa* was now rather inconveniently crowded by this reinforcement, but it was expected the voyage would not be a long one, though our destination was not as yet known. On the fourth morning after our embarkation, we were awakened early, by an extraordinary bustle on deck, which rather alarmed us; till some of the watch came hurrying down, to inform us that the wind had changed, and that the 'Blue Peter', the signal for sailing, was flying at the masthead of every vessel going with us. The intelligence was so gratifying to us as to produce, spontaneously, three hearty cheers. A gun was fired on board the agent [*admiral's*] ship, and the signal hoisted to get under way immediately.

The orders were so promptly obeyed, that in less than two hours we were out of the harbour, and passed some British men-of-war, who gave us some intimation of a storm that appeared to be brewing; the captains of our transports took the hint, and prepared for it, by lowering their topmasts and taking in some of their canvas. The prediction of the men-of-war was soon realized; the wind chopped round and blew with tremendous force; the waves ran so high that they were compelled to close the hatchways, leaving the men, women and children below, in utter darkness, and who therefore fancied the danger greater than it really was.

The North Sea is proverbial for its storms: and we had a good taste of them. As we could not proceed on our course, neither could we make any of the harbours for shelter, and were therefore compelled to keep knocking about for five days and nights, when we fortunately reached Yarmouth.

On the subsiding of the storm, we found all our vessels safe, except the brig we were at first on board, and which, unfortunately, went down the first day of the storm, and the crew all perished; thus, my application for removal was the means, under Providence, of saving the lives of the whole detachment.

We waited at Yarmouth a couple of days, to repair damages, and to lay in a stock of fresh provision; and the bum-boats which came were soon eased of their contents, and were kept employed in bring-

ing things on board as long as any money was left, when the men
began to barter the surplus portion of their dress.

Having disposed of my money before leaving Harwich, I was
anxious, like the rest, of laying in a stock, and recollecting there was
still a balance due to me, I made application for it to the officer who
had charge of the company, and he rather unceremoniously ordered
me to go about my business. I thought I was going about my business;
and this repulse did not deter me from reporting the circumstance
to the colonel, as soon as he came on deck; who immediately sent for
Lieutenant Browne,[1] and enquired the reason I was not settled with.
The lieutenant replied, that 'I *had* been settled with, before leaving
the depot'. The colonel asked 'if he had the books on board?' He
replied, 'they were', and was ordered to fetch them; and after going
through them, the colonel found there was a balance due to me, of
one pound eighteen shillings, which he was directed to pay instantly.
He said 'he had no money', and the paymaster just then coming on
deck, the colonel called out, 'Mr Williams,[2] let Mr Browne have a
little money.' The necessary sum was produced, and I was settled
with. The cash was soon disposed of; but, in pressing the claim, I
made an inveterate enemy of the officer, who was ever after on the
watch to do me an injury. All he was able to do, however, was to
prevent my promotion. I explained the awkwardness of my position
to the major, and he offered to remove me to some other company,
which I begged to decline; saying, 'I would do my duty, to the best
of my ability, and trust to the colonel and him for protection.'
Although I can forgive and forget an injury as well as any man living,
yet I really was hardly sorry when this officer, two years afterwards,
was mortally wounded.[3]

We now left Yarmouth with a perfectly fair wind, and without
any further delays reached the coast of Denmark when one of our
transports, the *Robert Harrison*, having part of the 91st regiment on
board ran aground, and fears were entertained for their safety; but
on the return of the tide, they were relieved from their perilous
position with but little damage.

We were at this time under convoy of the *Amphion* frigate; and on

[1] Donald Browne was then an Ensign. His promotion to Lieutenant was on 24 March
1814.

[2] John Williams was commissioned on 31 May 1810.

[3] Browne had his left arm amputated after Waterloo and died soon after.

entering the Belt to get to the Baltic Sea, we joined a fleet of merchantmen and kept company with them some distance. We were detained for some time in the Belt, by continual calms, and the prevalence of the thickest fog I ever saw; taking advantage of which a number of Danish gun-boats came out and fired on us, without however doing much injury. On one occasion we were progressing slowly and rather too near the Danish batteries, which opened on us, but were soon silenced by a few broadsides from the *Lion* seventy-four.

While we were becalmed here, the vessels were occasionally so close together that we could converse with each other; and having every bit of canvas spread, there being no wind, and the several regimental bands playing of an afternoon, the scene at such times was of the most imposing nature. The officers too, used to encourage games among the men, sometimes forming them in parties for dancing on deck; and having several boxes of oranges on board, they would throw them among the men, to produce a scramble. These various pastimes had the effect of keeping up a good understanding among the officers and men. There was one private soldier, named Ealy, on board, who, from his extraordinary likeness to Wellington, was called 'Lord Wellington', and in these sports he generally headed one of the parties, producing a great deal of amusement. From this trifling circumstance, I have no doubt had he afterwards conducted himself well, he would have been rapidly promoted; but in the first action we entered, he proved himself a rank coward, and the officers then turned their backs on him.

The monotony of the voyage was one morning rather unpleasantly relieved, by the infliction of corporal punishment. The officers had, by some means, obtained some fresh vegetables, and what was not consumed, was placed on the deck aft, under the charge of the sentry; the prisoner, who made free with a couple of carrots, was detected in the act, tried by a court-martial, and sentenced to receive one hundred and fifty lashes.

The morning the punishment took place, there was a stiff breeze, and the motion of the vessel prevented the drummers from always hitting one spot, so that the lashes fell sometimes on the back of the neck, then on the shoulders, and also over the back, which gave the man the appearance of having been very dreadfully punished, whereas in reality, he did not suffer so much as if he had been struck always on one place. However, as it was, it was considered quite unnecessary, and rather too severe for the offence; had they stopped his grog for a few days, it would have been quite sufficient.

These delays in our progress gave us ample time to reflect on our probable destiny. I have sat for hours together, meditating on my own folly or temerity, in thus rushing on to certain danger—perhaps to death. Of our regiment, consisting of about 30 officers and 550 men, how many of them were destined never to return? how many of them were to be disabled by severe wounds? and the question would arise—should I be among the first? or second? or should I return in safety?

The shots fired at us, on passing the Belt, had created rather uneasy sensations among us, being all young soldiers—not more than a dozen of us having ever before seen a shot fired in anger; and I must here confess that I felt the enthusiasm which had hitherto urged me on oozing out very fast; though I determined still to do my duty whatever dangers I might be exposed to.

Our officers on the whole seemed to be very soldierly. The colonel was the son of General [George] Harris, who gained so much celebrity and renown as commander of the Anglo-Indian forces at the storming of the important fortress of Seringapatam [1799]. The son had yet to be tried; but he had every appearance of being likely to do his duty. He had as fine a regiment under his command as any in the service, consisting chiefly of young men, from eighteen to thirty years of age, fit for any sort of duty.

Our light company was for the number, the finest set of men I ever saw, being a mixture of English, Irish and Scotch, commanded by a captain who had risen from the ranks. Report said, that he was indebted for his promotion, to his beautiful black eyes and whiskers, which had attracted the notice of his colonel's lady; who had sufficient influence to obtain for him a commission as ensign. He was now captain; and though his whiskers were tinged with grey, his eyes possessed all their former fire and brilliancy.

He was very eccentric in his ways; and his men scarcely knew how to please him. On one occasion, as we were going into action, one of the men excited his anger, and he ordered him to have an extra guard; and calling to his lieutenant, said, 'Reynolds,[1] if I am killed, see that Gorman has an extra guard.'—'Sergeant Pennyton!'—'Sir.'—'If Reynolds and I are killed, see that Gorman has an extra guard.'—'Yes,

[1] Thomas Reynolds, Lieutenant, 10 March 1814; wounded at Waterloo.

Sir.'—'None of your ready-made answers, Sir; but mind you do it, Sir!'—'Yes, Sir.'

On another occasion, he found a Bible in possession of one of the men, and ordered him to burn it; and made use of the following blasphemous expression: 'D——n you, Sir, I'll let you know that your firelock is your Bible, and I am your G—— a——!' With all his faults, however, he was a brave and well-disciplined officer.

His lieutenant, Reynolds, was a good little fellow; but was very unfortunate. If there was a shot fired at all, he was sure to get hit; while some men pass through so many fights without receiving a scratch.

The ensign of the light company, was a fine manly fellow named Loyd,[1] now a major in the service. He had sometimes to put up with the arbitrary conduct of his captain. Once, the latter said to him, 'D——n you, Sir, I'll let you know that I am your captain!' The ensign replied, 'And, Sir, you will please to recollect, at the same time, that I am Ensign Loyd, and a gentleman!'

By this time, we were acquainted with our destination, Swedish Pomerania, the Crown Prince having entered into a treaty with the British Government, whereby, on receiving one million of money, he engaged to join the Allied Sovereigns, with 80,000 Swedes; and it was intended that we should co-operate with him.

Our force consisted of the following regiments—the 25th, 33rd, 54th, 73rd, first Royals and 91st, amounting altogether to about 3,000 men; under the command of [*Major-*]General [*(Sir) Samuel*] Gibbs.[2]

In the latter part of August, we arrived at the island of Rugas [*Rügen*]; where we disembarked, and marched across the island to Stralsund—the place which acquired so much celebrity under the romantic Charles XII of Sweden. Our baggage, which took some time getting on shore—the ships not being able to come within half-a-mile of the beach—was afterwards conveyed by some small vessels up the river, and did not reach Stralsund till next day.

The whole of the troops were quartered on the inhabitants, and were very kindly treated by them: but for further particulars, I must refer the reader to the next chapter.

[1] John Y. Lloyd, Ensign; Lieutenant, 4 August 1814; wounded at Waterloo; Major, 20 March 1828.

[2] Mortally wounded at New Orleans in 1815.

II

Sound, sound the clarion! fill the fife,
To all the sensual world proclaim—
One crowded hour of glorious life
Is worth an age without a name!

The first morning after our arrival in Stralsund [*7 August 1813*], we discovered that our duties were likely to be of the most onerous, if not of the most dangerous, nature. The French General Morrand, had taken possession of it some few months before; and being called away suddenly, he destroyed most of the batteries and fortifications; and as there was a probability of its being now again attacked, it was necessary to place it in a state of defence. The Crown Prince who paid us a visit, drew off all the men capable of bearing arms, the tradesmen and wealthy burghers mounted guard at the town hall as private soldiers, and every man capable of labour was obliged to assist in repairing the batteries; we also were compelled to assist them; and there still being a deficiency of labourers, about a thousand young women, of the lower classes, were engaged, and dressed in male attire, were set to work, and were found very efficient; the women in that country being inured to field labour. Some ludicrous mistakes took place with some of our men, who in carrying on affairs of gallantry, were not always able to distinguish the women from the men.

Our duty now became very severe, as may be seen from the following statement for one week. Namely, Monday forenoon, attend parade at ten o'clock, eleven o'clock mount guard. Tuesday morning (at eleven) relieved from guard, go to quarters, change dress, and work for the rest of the day at the fortification. Wednesday, fall in two hours before daybreak, or as they say on service, 'until we can see a grey horse a mile': this was to prevent our being taken by surprise. Attend regimental parade at eleven; at eight o'clock in the evening fall in for picket; and patrol the streets till twelve. Go to quarters, get an hour or two rest; fall in two hours before daybreak on Thursday, get back to quarters by seven, attend regimental parade at ten, mount guard at eleven. Friday, relieved from guard at eleven, change dress and go to work. Saturday, fall in two hours before daybreak, attend parade at ten, work the rest of the day, picket at night. Sunday morning, fall in before daybreak as usual, parade at ten, mount guard at eleven.

Thus, it will be seen that we had very little time for rest; and we were so completely worn out, that one night, when I was placed as sentinel on a post of very considerable importance—although I knew the safety of the town depended on my vigilance—I could not resist the inclination to sleep; so, deliberately laying myself down on the ground, resting my firelock by my side, and placing a stone for my pillow, I fell asleep. Time passed quick; and I was awakened by a most terrific dream. An immense lion, I fancied was about springing on me. In the utmost terror I started to my feet, instinctively grasping my firelock, and heard footsteps approaching. I had sufficient presence of mind to give the usual challenge—'Who comes there?' and 'The Grand Round' was the reply. I demanded, 'Stand fast, Grand Round; advance sergeant, and give the countersign.' The sergeant advanced a few paces, pronounced the mystic word, and I called out, 'Pass on, Grand Round; all's well.'

It would not have been 'well' for me, had they caught me asleep; the inevitable punishment for such a crime under such circumstances would have been death. In a few minutes afterwards, the relieving sentinels came round, so that I had been asleep nearly two hours. I did not feel any more an inclination for sleep that night. I thanked God for my deliverance; and vowed never again to indulge in a nap while on sentry.

As the batteries were assuming a state of efficiency; and no tidings of the enemy, General Gibbs detached the 54th Regiment, to reconnoitre the country; and they had not been gone more than three or four days, when they returned in the utmost disorder; stating they had met with the enemy in considerable numbers, which induced them to make the best of their way back to Stralsund: and we, of course, expected the French would now pay us a visit. As there were still no signs of them, the General left Stralsund himself, taking only our regiment with him.

In Europe in 1813 political alignments and military operations were both fluid and complex. In broad terms, Wellington was in the process of driving the French out of Spain; Prussia and Russia were threatening Napoleon's

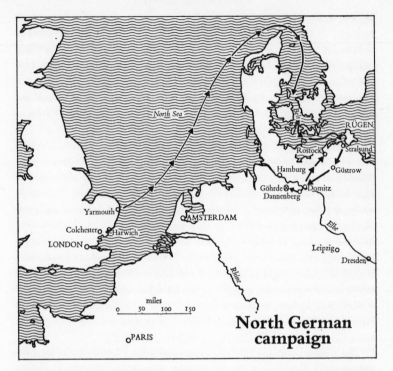

North German campaign

French and German troops[1] in Silesia and Saxony; Crown Prince Bernadotte[2] of Sweden was moving down on Napoleon from the north; and Austria under the guidance of its foreign minister, Metternich, on the plea of seeking 'armed mediation', was at the same time negotiating with Napoleon for peace, and preparing to join Prussia and Russia in a renewed struggle with France. The news of Wellington's victory at Vitoria (21 June) finally brought Austria into the war on the side of Prussia and Russia.

When this happened, Napoleon tried to hold forward positions and dispersed his forces to do so. Although he defeated the Allies at the Battle of Dresden (26 and 27 August), this dangerous dispersion proved his ruin. One of his corps was beaten near Berlin, a second corps was routed west of

[1] A great many of Napoleon's troops were recruited from the German states of the Rhine.

[2] Bernadotte was one of Napoleon's marshals who changed sides. In 1810 he had been elected Crown Prince of Sweden and heir to the throne, and with Charles XIII's health failing, the reins of government came into his hands. He became King of Sweden as Charles XIV in 1818.

Breslau, and a third was defeated south of Dresden at Kulm (30 August) in Bohemia. In five days Napoleon lost 100,000 men, the best of his artillery and most of his baggage. Even Marshal Ney, 'the bravest of the brave', was totally defeated when he was sent north towards Berlin, losing 25,000 men and 80 guns. Then when the troops under Napoleon's personal command, who might have won battles, advanced, the Allies cleverly fell back and disengaged, so that after three fruitless marches of this kind Napoleon returned to Dresden in disgust.

✓ *In the north-west the Hanoverian General Walmoden with a mixed force of his own countrymen, Swedes, Russians, the 73rd Regiment from Britain and half a British rocket-battery, the whole numbering about 20,000 men, moved successfully against the isolated French corps under Davout on the lower Elbe, south-east of Hamburg. Sergeant Morris was with the 73rd, and, as a participant, describes the little known battle of Göhrde, forty-five, miles south-east of Hamburg. Fortescue says of it: 'On the 16th of September, a portion of Walmoden's force beat one of Davout's detachments handsomely at Göhrde, killing and wounding 2,000 of the French, capturing 15,000 prisoners and 8 guns, and compelling the Marshal, against the whole tenor of Napoleon's plans, to stand on the defensive in isolation from the main French army'; adding in a footnote, 'The British 73rd and half of the rocket-battery were present at the action but suffered no casualties.'*

The decisive moment of the campaign came when Blücher crossed the Elbe and attacked Napoleon north of Leipzig. Russia and Austria also came against him from the east and south, and there was fought at Leipzig one of the most bloody and decisive battles of all time (16–19 October). In the battle 300,000 Allied troops attacked 180,000 troops under Napoleon, over twice the total engaged at Waterloo two years later. The French loss is reckoned at 68,000, 30,000 killed and 38,000 prisoners; that of the Allies at 52,000; casualties double those of the later battle. After three days of desperate fighting Napoleon was driven westward with the wreck of his army, leaving some of his best troops locked up in the fortresses of Germany. Forsaken by his main German allies, the Bavarians and Saxons, soon all Germany turned against him. He crossed the Rhine and reached France in November 1813.

As is recorded in the text, Sergeant Morris expresses regret at not being present at the great battle of Leipzig. He felt compensated, however, by being present at Waterloo.

We left Swedish Pomerania, and proceeded through Germany, by forced marches, of about thirty miles a day; and as we had no

Commissary with us, we were obliged to trust entirely to chance for our daily supplies. In the various towns through which we passed, more particularly at Güstrow, the inhabitants behaved towards us with the greatest kindness, striving with each other which should have the honour of entertaining us.

Our journey, after leaving the last-named town, was through a country purely agricultural; and yet, though it was in the beginning of September, there were no signs of harvest. The country had been overrun with troops, alternately friendly and hostile; but (whether one or the other) draining them of their resources, driving away their cattle, and producing the utmost desolation; so that though the inhabitants of the villages were extremely kind to us, it was not in their power to furnish us with any provision, even for money. The only inhabitants indeed remaining in the villages, were old men and women, and young children, no cattle, no horses, sheep, pigs or poultry; the trees, indeed, were yielding abundance of fruit, and there were a few tobacco fields in cultivation: with these exceptions, it is impossible to describe the state of desolation to which the country had been reduced.

Though General Gibbs left Stralsund with us, he did not accompany us always. He was desirous of falling in with some of the allied troops. Napoleon was at this time at Dresden, with upwards of 100,000 men. Murat, Ney, Davout and some others of the French marshals were occupying strong positions between Dresden and Leipsic, ready to act singly, or co-operate with their master, as circumstances might require. Against these, were the combined forces of Austria, Russia and Prussia and the Crown Prince, with 30,000 Swedes. The utmost reliance was now placed in the fidelity and ability of Bernadotte; and he was created Generalissimo of the Allied Troops.

Our regiment continued to advance, though with what object was not known. The weather was very hot; and for a whole week we had nothing to subsist on but such potatoes or fruit as we could pick up on the march; generally bivouacking in a wood, at night.

On 15 September, towards the close of the day when our colonel was looking out for some suitable spot on which to pass the night, and pointing to a wood in the distance as seeming to promise the necessary accommodation; having nearly reached the spot—whether through the ignorance or treachery of our guide, I know not—but we found ourselves within two miles of the French camp, of 20,000 men. Had they been aware of our approach, they could have detached two or three regiments of cavalry and have taken the whole of us prisoners. As soon as we found out our mistake, we lost but little time in placing ourselves at a more respectful distance. Having gone about five miles in another direction, we fell in with General Walmoden, with about 20,000 Germans and Hanoverians; and though night was drawing on, he was breaking up his camp to attack the enemy, whom we were so close upon.

We were now fortunate enough to get a supply of bread, and two cows, alive; they were soon dispatched however, and cut up after a manner—some of the men roasting their portions at the wood fires, and some actually devouring it raw—warm, as it came from the beast, after the Abyssinian fashion.

After two or three hours' rest, we also were ordered to advance, but not exactly in the track of our allies. They crossed the Elbe, at Dormitz [Domitz], and we proceeded to Dannenberg, where the enemy had broken down the bridge, and it was midnight before a bridge of boats could be constructed to enable us to pass. How we got over I cannot tell; for we were so thoroughly fatigued, that we actually slept as we walked along. Towards morning we were indulged with about two hours' repose, on the grass; when we were again urged forward.

General Count Walmoden had overtaken and engaged the enemy, on the plains of Gordo [Göhrde], in Hanover, about fifteen miles from our last town. As soon as we heard firing we were hurried on to assist, and went double-quick through the wood—in which we passed a delightful country seat, the property of George III, as Elector of Hanover; and soon afterwards, emerging from the wood a most extraordinary sight presented itself to us.

On our left was the French army, drawn up with their right near the wood. On their right centre was a hill on which some cannon with a strong body of infantry, were placed. On their extreme left was a solid square of French infantry; and as we entered the field, the latter were attacked by some of our cavalry, consisting of the 2nd and 3rd German Hussars [King's German Legion]. The attack was not successful; the cavalry were repulsed with considerable loss.

As soon as Walmoden perceived us, he rode up with a couple of aides-de-camp. His appearance, for a general—especially for a general commanding in a field of battle—was the most extraordinary I have ever seen. He was actually smoking one of the long German pipes, the flexible tube passing round his body, and the bowl deposited in a pouch, by his horse's side. Addressing our commanding officer, he said, 'Colonel, I am glad you are come; I want that hill taken!' pointing to the one with the two pieces of cannon, and about a thousand men on it. 'Will you charge them, Colonel?' 'Yes, Sir,' was the answer. 'Well,' said the German, 'I shall send a Hanoverian regiment to assist you.' On which our colonel observed, 'Let us try it ourselves, General, first; and if we fail, then assist us.' Then, addressing the regiment, he said, 'Now, my lads, you see what we have to do; we are the only regiment of English in the field: don't let us disgrace ourselves!' A hearty cheer from the men was the assurance that they would do their duty. The colonel, calling the quartermaster, told him to endeavour to get us a supply of schnaps, by the time we had done the job; and then he led us on to the foot of the hill. As we began to ascend, the enemy fired one volley, which being ill-directed, passed over us harmless, or nearly so; and then they abandoned their position, and retreated, on perceiving the English colours, which our officers had just unfurled; previously, they were rolled up in oilskin cases.

In order to account for this apparent cowardice on the part of the French, their general, himself, informed us afterwards, when taken prisoner, that when he was attacked by the Hanoverians, the whole being in British uniform, he had a difficulty in persuading his men that they were not English; and when our regiment began to ascend the hill, they, of course, took us to be part of the Hanoverians; but when the British colours were exhibited, the French troops fancied that not only we, but the majority of the red coats were English, and this circumstance caused such a panic among his men, that he could no longer keep them to their duty.

The French right, on seeing the hill abandoned, fled also. The square of French infantry on the left, which I have before alluded to, were still firm; but there happened to be two or three of the Rocket Brigade in the field, and the first rocket fired, fell directly in the square, putting them in the greatest confusion; and while they were so, the German Hussars, who had been previously repulsed, charged them again, and influenced by feelings of revenge, cut among them, right and left, giving no quarter.

The French were now defeated at all points, and the result was about 800 French killed, 1,200 wounded, and 1,500 prisoners; our loss in killed and wounded, was about 800. This battle is very slightly mentioned in history, and no notice whatever has been taken of our presence. If it had been a battalion of the Guards so engaged, the circumstance would have found a prominent place in history; but as it was only a paltry regiment of the line, of course it was not worth recording, as there was nothing in the shape of patronage to be secured by it.

I have stated that the French General was taken prisoner, and there was a circumstance connected with his capture worth recording. Finding his efforts to rally his men ineffectual, being wounded, he endeavoured to make good his own retreat but was closely pursued by one of the 2nd German Hussars. The General, in order to check him in the pursuit, threw on the ground a well-filled purse. The hussar noticed the spot where the purse fell, but continued the pursuit, when the General surrendered, and on retracing their steps the German dismounted, took up the purse and gave it to the General: who, when he met our General, reported the brave and disinterested conduct of the man. General Gibbs, who arrived in the field during the action, was so struck with the conduct of the hussar, that he attached him to his own person as an orderly, and when that general was killed afterwards at New Orleans, in America, the man was found dead by his side.

In the course of this engagement, we were joined by a Regiment of Russian Cossacks; a set of barbarians, inspiring as much terror in our own ranks as in those of the enemy. There was nothing like discipline preserved by them, and their principal object seemed to be plunder, no matter how obtained, whether from friend or foe. One of them having killed a man, was in the act of stripping him, when another came up to assist him, 'No, no! my good friend', said the first one, 'go and kill a man for yourself.' They did not confine themselves to taking watches, money, or other valuables, but stripped the dead and dying of every particle of clothing, taking with them such as they thought worth carrying, and scattering the rest about the ground.

Having collected the prisoners, to the amount of 1,500, who were placed under our charge, we paid such attention to the wounded as circumstances would admit of, and there being no town nearer than the one we last left, and the weather extremely wet, we made the best arrangement we could for the night; and miserable indeed was our position. The rain continued the whole night, increasing tenfold the sufferings of the wounded, and rendering our situation anything but pleasant.

Notwithstanding these unpleasant circumstances however, such was our state of exhaustion that no sooner were the prisoners arranged, being surrounded by sentinels with orders to shoot any of them who should endeavour to escape, than the rest of us laid down and slept on the ground, exposed to the 'pelting of the pitiless storm'. At daybreak next morning the weather cleared up, and we were engaged for an hour or two in lighting fires and drying ourselves. A number of wagons arrived from Dannenberg for the removal of the wounded, and we had to escort the prisoners to that place. Some of them had been in English prisons, and seemed pleased when it was intimated to them that they would be sent to England, by which we may suppose they had been tolerably well treated there. On our arrival at Dannenberg, the prisoners were placed under a guard in the Town Hall, and the wounded French, as they arrived, were deposited on straw in the pews of the church.

General Gibbs was here with us, and we were billeted on the inhabitants. I obtained tolerably good quarters; but just as I had got something to eat, and was about to retire to rest on some clean straw, (there being so many of us, beds were out of the question) I was called out on what is called 'fatigue duty', and our employment during the whole of the night was assisting the surgeons in the church, who had taken their station near the altar; and we carried to them such of the wounded as were marked for amputation, holding them while the operation was performed, and then depositing them on the floor with straw to lie on, and an allowance of bread and water to each; and occasionally, carrying away such of them as had died, to the holes prepared in the yard for them. In the morning there was a stack of amputated limbs beside the altar, which we had afterwards to remove and bury.

On leaving this place we were relieved from the charge of the prisoners, where they were taken to I never could learn. We returned by the same road through Germany, and were exposed to the same privations until we had passed Güstrow, when, as on our advance, we subsisted on the inhabitants; instead of going back to Stralsund, we diverged to the left, and went to Rostock in Mecklenburgh, where we obtained very comfortable quarters.

During our stay at Rostock, the reigning Prince of Mecklenburgh returned to his palace, a splendid building, situated at the end of the principal street; and a series of entertainments were given to celebrate the release of Germany from the thraldom of the ambitious Napoleon.

Notwithstanding the desolation of the surrounding country, the town of Rostock seemed to be amply supplied with provisions, of every sort; and to us they appeared remarkably cheap. At an eating-house near the Town Hall, I have frequently got an excellent dinner, consisting of poultry, fish, and flesh, with abundance of vegetables, and a glass of schnaps included, for threepence halfpenny. Geese, here, are remarkably good and plentiful; a good sized one could be had at the cook-shop, ready dressed, for 1s. 3d. A great many of the inhabitants of this and other towns in Germany keep geese, which I suppose by some municipal regulation, are taken out every morning to feed on the commons. The man who takes charge of them, goes through the town in the morning blowing a horn, on hearing which the keepers of geese turn them out. When all are collected, they are taken to the common: and at night the man brings them back to the owners. A similar practice prevails in regard to the pigs which are summoned by the cracking of a whip, and taken in like manner to the common. The abundance of geese enables the people to indulge in the luxury of the the finest feather beds, one under, and one over them, with a pair of sheets only between them.

I had the good fortune to be quartered here upon a very respectable Lutheran minister, whose house was adjoining the church. He could speak a little English; and I understood, by this time, something of the German; and every morning, when I was off duty, he would invite me into his library: when the servant used invariably to bring us in two buns, and two glasses of rum, and he would question me about England, its customs, politics, religion, and so on, occasionally referring to some of his books. After passing an hour thus, he would dress and go to the church, to perform his religious duties. The short time I passed in the house of this worthy pastor, was about the most agreeable that I have ever experienced.

The latter end of October the frost set in with the great severity, and the weather-wise then predicted that we should have a long and severe winter.

On the arrival of the transports, we left Rostock amidst the strongest manifestations of goodwill and friendship from the inhabitants; and after a march of a few miles, we reached the shores of the Baltic, in the Gulf of Lubec. This was on the 2nd of November 1813; the sea was uncommonly rough, and the process of embarkation was both difficult and dangerous. Having none but the ships' boats, it was late at night before the various regiments got on board; and then some of the officers were obliged to leave their horses behind them.

The two vessels in which our regiment embarked were the *Ajax* and *Mountaineer*, rickety things, of about 400 tons each. The wind increased in violence, and we were buffeted about at the mercy of the waves for two days and nights; every wave dashing over the vessel, compelling us to keep the hatchways closed, and the watch, on deck, obliged to lash themselves to some part of the vessel, to prevent them from being washed overboard.

As it was found impossible to proceed, in such weather, we sought shelter in the harbour of Gottenburg; where we were detained for fourteen days. This delay was very distressing, as the majority of our men were attacked with dysentery; and the effluvia between deck was so horribly offensive and insupportable, that those who were free from the disorder (and I was fortunately one of them) chose rather to remain, day and night, on deck, sleeping in or under the long-boat, in the forecastle, or anywhere that we could stow ourselves away; the frost at the time being so intense, that the ships were actually frozen in. A Lieutenant Dowling,[1] and another officer, belonging to us, were sent up the river to Gottenburg, where they were detained for a fortnight; and spent—for their own subsistence—the money with which they had been provided to purchase some necessary things for the men.

When released from this place, we had a favourable, though rather brisk, wind; and in four days we reached Yarmouth Roads, where we were exposed to another tremendous storm, which continued, with fearful violence, through the night. When daylight appeared, seventeen vessels were discovered on shore, some of them complete wrecks.

We hoped, having so much sickness on board, that we should be permitted to land directly; but had to await the arrival of instructions from the Government, which, when they came, were a sad disappointment to many. The order was—the whole of the women and children[2] should be left on shore, at Yarmouth, and the troops sent directly to Holland; and it was expected our landing there would be strongly contested by the French. These orders were a sad disappointment to most of us; but it was particularly distressing to the married people, to be separated thus suddenly—the women and

---

[1] [*Joseph Dowling, Lieutenant, 13 August 1812.*] This officer is now Barrack-master at the Wellington Barracks, London. [*T.M.*]

[2] It was quite customary for the women and children to accompany the regiment in campaigns. Some took part in the retreat to Corunna.

children landed in a strange place, perhaps hundreds of miles from their home, and no resources; the men, most of them ill, on board, with the prevailing disorder. But the orders were imperative, and so, after getting in a supply of fresh provisions, we left Yarmouth with a fair wind, and in a few hours made the coast of Holland.

On 12 December, we reached Helvoetsluys [*Hellevoetsluis*], which had just been evacuated by the French. We proceeded up the river to Williamstadt [*Willemstad*], which was also just abandoned by the enemy; and we had the opportunity of landing without any interruption. It was fortunate for us, that such was the case, as most of our men were so dreadfully weakened by the disorder, that it was with the utmost difficulty they were got on shore; and they were instantly sent into the hospital. However, a few days' judicious treatment, with proper diet, and medicines, put them to rights, and we soon began again to assume an appearance of efficiency. The illness I have alluded to was confined to our regiment, and was supposed to have been produced by our excessive fatigue, and bad living, throughout Germany. The other portion of the troops had remained all the time in quarters, at Stralsund; where, after we left, the duty was tolerable, as the works were completed; and having correct information of the operations of the contending armies, they were no longer under any apprehensions of an attack.

Our regiment cut rather a miserable figure beside the other regiments in another respect. They having been in a state of comparative inactivity, had preserved their regimental dresses in good order; while ours, from our bivouacking in the woods, and marching a distance of upwards of 300 miles, were in such a shattered condition, that many of the men had their red coats mended with the grey trouser cloth, there being no possibility of obtaining any red cloth for the purpose. But though the others could boast of a superiority in appearance, all the honour rested with us.

In again alluding to the battle of Gorde, it will be perceived, that the enemy we defeated, had been detached on a most important duty; namely, to open the passage for the French troops to Magdeburg. The consequence of our victory was, that the French General, Davout, was not able to carry into effect his plan of reaching that place; and without arrogating too much to ourselves, I think our regiment may consider the panic caused by the appearance of their colours, was the means of rendering the victory more decisive than it would otherwise have been.

Should it be supposed that I have exaggerated the fears of the French, on the appearance of the English colours, I could adduce two more instances, in which the French have contended well with us, before they discovered that we were English, when they instantly fled. But the fact I have already alluded to, can be attested by respectable parties now living. There are two officers now resident in this metropolis, who were present; the one is Major Mead, who then belonged to us, and was aide-de-camp to General Gibbs; he exchanged from us into the 21st Fusiliers, and very sorry we were to lose him, for he was, in every sense of the word, an officer and a gentleman. He holds now an appointment in the Adjutant-General's office, at the Horse Guards. Captain Dowling was present; and would, I have no doubt, bear testimony to the truth of my observations.

I believe, the reason why our presence in that engagement was not noticed at the time, was, that the general (Gibbs) had exceeded his instructions in carrying us so far. I am sorry he did not take us a little farther, as I should much like to have witnessed the grand operations before Leipsic;—not that I am, by any means, fond of slaughter; but there was something so very interesting in the capture of Leipsic, that I have often wished I had been there. It will appear, from the subsequent chapters of this narrative, that I was afterwards called on to witness some scenes, quite as grand in their development, and quite as glorious in their results.

III

Red Battle stamps his foot,
And Nations feel the shock.

In November 1813 the people of Amsterdam rose up in rebellion against their French masters and proclaimed the House of Orange with the cry of 'Orange Boven'. Other towns followed their example, and a provisional government was established in the name of the Prince of Orange and Nassau. The people appeared enthusiastic although unorganized and lacking in arms with which to capture the fortresses held by the French, the strongest of which was Bergen-op-Zoom. Accordingly the British Government decided to send immediate aid, and a small force under Lieutenant-General Sir Thomas Graham of Barrosa fame was despatched to Holland to their help. It was this force of which the 73rd Regiment with Sergeant Morris was a part.

Whereas the French were concentrated in fortresses like Bergen-op-Zoom and Antwerp, the Allies were widely scattered. The Russians were at Breda, the Prussians at Bommel, and the British, having landed at Hellevoetsluis and on Tholen Island, were assembled at Willemstad (see map, p.31).

Early in the year 1814, in wintry weather, the village of Merxem on the outskirts of Antwerp was captured; but as the weather became increasingly cold, with cutting winds sweeping over the marshes; and as the troops had no warm clothing, General Graham moved them back to winter quarters around Westwesel, half way between Antwerp and Bergen-op-Zoom.

In February in better weather, a second attack on Merxem was made; but then it turned suddenly cold again. The winter in fact was the coldest in living memory—in London the Thames was frozen over. In this second assault the Duke of Clarence was present; and in the forefront of the battle apparently, for he is reported as getting a bullet through the skirt of his coat.

Once Merxem had fallen for the second time, General Graham took his royal visitor up into the belfry of a church to have a good look at Antwerp. The sight of enemy shipping lying apparently at his mercy in the basin of the Scheldt made him decide on a bombardment. This however proved value-less. What with indifferent shooting and shells which failed to explode, the damage done to the enemy vessels was negligible.

Changing his plan, Graham turned his attention to Bergen-op-Zoom; and there followed the unfortunate attack on Bergen-op-Zoom (in March 1814) which Sergeant Morris criticizes.

Everything went wrong. The French got news of the coming attack and the value of surprise was lost. Then the British attack, owing to mistakes by Graham's generals, was made piecemeal and at the wrong time. Even when 3000 British troops managed to fight their way into the fortress, many of them pushed on too far and got themselves cut off from the main body so that they were forced to surrender. Then the French, encouraged by this, fought back so successfully that all the bastions won by the British were recaptured in turn. In the end the remaining British who were not captured scrambled out of the fortress in disorder, much to the disgust of General Graham whose reserves had arrived too late to salvage what should have been a victory.

The regiments composing our brigade, left Williamstadt on 28 December. There was a partial breaking of the frost; and our first day's march was the most miserable I have ever experienced. The roads were literally knee-deep in mud; many lost their shoes and boots. After toiling all day, we were only able to accomplish a distance of about ten miles, when we were quartered on the inhabitants of a village; and though the people were poor, they treated us kindly, and there appeared among them an apparently sincere desire to be released from French domination.

The Stadtholder, or Prince of Orange, had been driven from his country eighteen years before, when the French republican forces proceeded triumphantly through Belgium, entered Holland, drove the army commanded by the Duke of York, from one town to another, until at length, they were compelled (at least, what was left of them) to abandon the country, which immediately fraternised with the French. But they were now heartily sick of them, and anxious for the restoration of the former dynasty. This revolution in favour of the Prince of Orange, was as unexpected to that Prince, as it was to the French; who not anticipating such an event, had drawn off a portion of the several garrisons to reinforce the army; when the people spontaneously, as it were, rose in several places, drove out the French troops, and proclaimed the Prince of Orange.

The French Emperor was now placed in a position so extremely critical, that his overthrow seemed inevitable, unless he should succeed in making some pacific arrangements with the Allied Sovereigns, who had now hemmed him in on every side; and, possessing such advantages, they were not likely to consent to any terms short of the complete restoration of all those places, which had been taken by the French since the Revolution, as well as to obtain some guarantee against future aggressions.

The chief command of the force concentrating in Holland, was given to Sir Thomas Graham; an appointment which gave universal satisfaction to the troops. It was some time, however, before we saw or heard anything of him.

The frost having set in with increased severity, put a stop to our operations; and we were quartered on the various towns and villages, and received from England an ample supply of stores, including the year's regimental dress (not before we wanted it), with an abundance of flannel shirts, thick worsted stockings, and such other things as were necessary to protect us from the inclemency of a winter in Holland; bearing in mind, probably, the horrible sufferings of the British troops, when last there, under the Duke of York [1795].

There was at least a probability of our being involved in similar disasters, as all the strongly-fortified places were still in possession of the enemy; and notwithstanding the recent reverses of the Emperor Napoleon, Belgium being in his possession, he could, in a short time, march a sufficient number of troops to Holland, to drive us back to our ships; and his troops, especially those in garrison, were as enthusiastically attached to him as ever.

Notwithstanding the severity of the weather, we left the pretty town of Rosendall [Roosendaal] and advanced through the country in the direction of Antwerp; the intention of General Graham was to cut off the communication between that place and Bergen-op-Zoom, as well as to deprive each of them from drawing their usual supplies from the surrounding country.

Acting on some information which had been received, we made a forced march, to intercept a body of French troops, intended to reinforce Bergen-op-Zoom. We took up our position on a common, on the line of road which they were expected to traverse, and waited for them some hours, exposed to the drifting snow, and a bitter north-east wind. Some dragoons were dispatched in search of the enemy; and on their return, we learned that the French had been already encountered, and beaten, by some of the Dutch troops, at Westwesel. After this disappointment, we separated, and sought shelter from the cold. Our commissariat arrangements were as yet tolerably good, the bread and meat being served out with the utmost regularity;

The Netherlands

but the food, if not eaten directly, became frozen so very hard, as to require great force to break it, and I have seen a piece of meat actually freezing on one side, while it was frying on the other—that was when they were cooking their meat at the fire, lit on the ground, in the open air.

The cottagers whom we were billeted on, were so very poor, that very few indeed had the second bed; and all we could expect from them was potatoes and tobacco, both grown by themselves, and for which, they generally received from us an equivalent in meat, which was to them a great luxury. Their dinner generally consisted of a large bowl of potatoes, they always selecting the smallest for their own use, and giving the large ones to the cows or pigs. Over the potatoes, when boiled, they poured some sweet oil and vinegar, and this, with some very brown bread, was their usual fare. There was a fork laid for each person, and they used their own clasp knives. When the oil used, was really sweet, I was rather fond of their mess. On Sundays they generally had a piece of bacon with their potatoes. Such of them as indulged in the use of coffee, had a very small cup, something like

31

what the children in England play with. Sugar was a prohibited article, and as a substitute for it, they would put a piece of sugar candy in the mouth, to sweeten the coffee in its passage. After each meal, the whole of the family produce their pipes, and taking from the pouch—which they invariably carry with them—a portion of their home-grown tobacco, after cutting it in small pieces, and rolling it in their hands, they would fill their pipes, and indulge in the luxury of smoking; in which habit even the children indulge. Even if we, by good fortune, obtained possession of a bed, we had the most imperative orders not to undress; and in some instances, indeed, we were prohibited from taking off our accoutrements: and every morning, whatever might be the state of the weather, we were compelled to be under arms an hour or two before daybreak. All these measures were adopted, to prevent our being taken by surprise by the enemy.

Severe as the weather was, we were continually on the move, and to add to the unpleasantness of our journey, the French had opened the sluices, and inundated the country to a very considerable extent; and as the waters increased, successive layers of ice were formed, of which the top surface not always being sufficiently strong to bear us, we would go down to the next and have to wade through the water: and whenever we came to dry ground, or firm ice, the trousers would instantly freeze, making them uncomfortable for the rest of the journey. The hardships we suffered in these marches, would be sufficient to kill any solitary traveller, but there being a large body of us together, we kept each other alive.

On 26 January 1814, being within five miles of Antwerp, we fell in with a body of the French troops, and immediately engaged them, and as they fought rather obstinately, Sir Thomas Graham ordered us to retire and roll up our greatcoats, which, on account of the extreme cold, we had been permitted to wear with the accoutrements over them, and it was thought the French had thus mistaken us for raw Dutch troops. There seemed to be some truth in this, for on our again advancing the enemy immediately fled, and we pursued them even to the gates of Antwerp; but, as they opened upon us from the batteries, we, in our turn, were forced to retire.

It was thought that General Graham had received some intimation that the inhabitants of Antwerp, who were known to be favourable to us, intended to open the gates and assist us in expelling the French garrison; but while the brave and celebrated French General Carnot had possession of the citadel, they would not dare to do so, as he could have destroyed the whole town in two days. Indeed, it was to overawe the city that the citadel was built, by the Spanish General Alva, at the time the Netherlands formed a part of the possessions of Spain.

The French garrison of Brada [*Breda*] was about this time defeated by stratagem. A regiment of Cossacks approached the gates, and avowing themselves to be the advanced guard of 10,000 Russians, struck such consternation among the French, that they immediately evacuated the place, leaving six hundred of their number as prisoners in the hands of their brave assailants. When the French found out how they had been cheated, they made an effort to recover the place, but the Cossacks, aided most willingly by the citizens, repulsed them with considerable loss.

A circumstance connected with our recent brush before Antwerp, created some amusement afterwards. The drum-major of a regiment in our brigade, who, though he had not been within the smell of powder, wrote an eloquent and affectionate letter to his wife in London, giving her a detailed (but purely imaginary) account of the affair, describing very minutely his own exploits; how, that, when his regiment was ordered to charge, he rushed on and succeeded in taking with his own hands one of the enemy's standards; that he had received several wounds, none of them, however, dangerous; and that the circumstance was witnessed by his commanding officer, who had reported it to Sir Thomas Graham, and he expected, of course to be rewarded with a commission. The receipt of such a letter could not but be highly pleasing to the good wife, who took occasion to show it to some of her friends, who advised her to send it to the editor of one of the daily papers, who immediately gave it insertion, and in a very short time a copy found its way to the mess-table of the regiment to which the man belonged. The officers, after a hearty laugh at the 'Bombastes Furioso' qualities of their drum-major, gave the paper to the men, and the circumstance became known through the brigade. The poor fellow was for ever afterwards pestered with enquiries as to when he expected his commission?

The weather continuing very severe, we were divided among the number of villages, and iron-bound as the ground was with the frost, we threw up some strong entrenchments, embracing Calnthoupt [*Calmhout*], Brecht and Westwesel, thus rendering ourselves tolerably secure from a surprise from the garrison, either of Antwerp or Bergen-op-Zoom. The latter end of January another move was made towards Antwerp, and having been strongly reinforced by some heavy artillery and some large-sized mortars, there was no doubt now of something serious being in contemplation.

On the night of 1 February, our brigade took up the advanced position at a village called Donk, about five or six miles from Antwerp, and only two miles from the enemy's advanced posts. This village contained about 100 houses and a good many barns, the latter being our most favourite lodgings, provided we had plenty of straw; as, by lying closely together, we contrived to keep away the cold. I had the good fortune here to be quartered on a large château, and though we were strictly prohibited from injuring the property of the inhabitants of the country, yet this seat being known to be the private property of the French General, was devoted to destruction. A large fire was made on the hearth of the drawing-room, fed by the valuable furniture, which was broken up for the purpose. Some very valuable paintings and looking-glasses were wantonly destroyed.

Before daybreak, we fell in with the utmost silence. The snow had fallen heavily in the night, and still continued; nevertheless, we were ordered to advance. A young man, belonging to us, made rather an extraordinary request to the officer, viz. that he might be placed on the baggage guard, as he had received an intimation, by a dream, that if he went on, he would be the first man killed. Of course, his request was not complied with; and we endeavoured to laugh him out of his fears, but in vain. We were soon discovered by the enemy; who, in the first instance, opened on us some of their light artillery. The first shot that took effect, was a six-pounder, which struck poor Francis, whose dream was thus unhappily realised—he was the first man killed.

On our further advance, we met with some serious obstructions. The enemy had very strongly entrenched themselves behind some trees, which had been cut down for the purpose, and placed across the road: the wind being against us, drifted such large quantities of snow, as literally to blind us. Being still exposed to the enemy's fire, the order was given to force the entrenchment; and instantly rushing forward, we drove the enemy before us, until we reached the main street of the village of Merxem, when they rallied, and opened on us two pieces of cannon, with grape-shot, which compelled us to seek shelter from the sides and gable-ends of the houses. Upon this, Lieutenant [*John*] Acres,[1] of our Grenadiers—more familiarly known as 'Bob Acres', a man of gigantic stature, as brave as a lion, and almost

[1] Lieutenant 20 November 1811. 'Bob Acres' was the country squire in Sheridan's *The Rivals*, first produced in 1775.

34

as strong as one—rushing into the middle of the street, called on us to follow him; nor did he call in vain. In a moment, every man was after him. We drove the enemy from the main street, took the two pieces of cannon, and pursued the foe up one of the side streets. They were followed up to the gates of Antwerp; the distance from the village to that town is two miles and a half.

The light brigade which made this attack, consisted of the following regiments: the 25th, 33rd, 52nd, 73rd and 95th Rifles. Our regiment took a different direction to the other, perceiving some two or three hundred of the French diverging to the left, from the road. If the ground had been passable, this would have been a nearer road to the town; but there was now a broad sheet of water, in which about forty of them boldly entered: the rest gave themselves up as prisoners, throwing their firelocks down in a heap.

The company I belonged to, was ordered to continue the pursuit of these in the water, which was frozen over, but not sufficiently strong to bear. Both the enemy, and ourselves, therefore, had to break the ice as we waded through the water, which was about three feet deep; and as the French refused to surrender, we continued to fire on them, until there was not more than five or six left; and they effected their escape.

On our return to the village, we were surprised at the number of our troops which had come up, consisting of the heavy brigade, among whom were some of the Foot Guards.

The batteries of the town now opened on us a well-directed and destructive fire; notwithstanding this, we succeeded in forming several batteries, and began to exchange a few shots with them. Their principal aim was the village, as they knew we were there in considerable numbers. Many of the houses were set on fire by the shells, and more of them were battered by the shot.

The inhabitants had most of them retired to the city for safety, taking with them such portions of their property as they could remove. I observed one house, the owner of which had remained, who professed himself friendly to us. His house, however, like the rest, was knocked down by the shot. I was several hours before I had an opportunity of drying my clothes, and then only by standing before a wood fire, that was lit on the ground. Our daily supply of schnaps we found of considerable service; it was served out in camp-kettles, each man receiving about a third of a pint, which they generally put out of sight at once, in order to make sure of it.

That night I was on an outline picket, patrolling the ground in advance towards the town. It was a beautiful night, but very cold; as we passed along, the apparent desolation caused in so short a time was surprising! On coming to the house I have before alluded to, where the man had remained, we noticed that in the demolition of the building most of the materials had fallen forward into the street; and as I had been in the house in the daytime, and noticed the situation of the door, it struck me that, by clearing away some of the timber from the back part, we might gain an entrance to the cellar, and obtain from thence something to warm us. After about an hour's labour, we were successful in clearing a way to the lower part of the building, and were much surprised, and rather startled, to hear sounds proceeding from thence. On going down, we found the man, with his whole family, had retired there for safety, and by the destruction of the house had been buried alive; and there they would probably have remained, but for our exertion. They were very grateful for their deliverance, and readily gave us what had been the object of our search.

The troops were all under arms the whole of that night, and before daybreak took up their respective position for the ensuing day. The town batteries recommenced firing about six o'clock, and then balls followed each other in rapid succession. During the forenoon Sir Thomas Graham entered Merxem, accompanied by the Duke of Clarence, who, to witness the operations, obtained a seat in the belfry of the church; and remained there until a shot from the enemy struck the steeple, and gave him an intimation that his royal person was not exactly safe; he immediately descended, mounted his horse, and rode off to the rear.

Our regiment was engaged, in the face of the enemy, in constructing a sand-bag mortar battery, which is formed as follows:— Such a number of men, as may be deemed sufficient, are provided each with a canvas bag, which is to be filled with sand and secured at the mouth by a string. These are then deposited in rows, under the superintendence of the artillery-men, and in an hour or two a battery may be so formed, which will bear a great deal of battering. Having completed our job, the mortars were brought up, fixed, and commenced firing. It must not be supposed, however, that we had been doing all this unobserved by the enemy from the town, or that we did not receive from them some very striking intimations of their displeasure at our bold advances. Fortunately for us, there happened to be a mound of earth which screened us from their shot, while we lay down; we had to remain on this spot, not only through the day but during the following night; and, as the evening drew in, we began to dig caves to keep off a portion of the cold air, as well as a shelter from the shot. The ground being chiefly sand, we were enabled to do this with the aid of some pickaxes and shovels, the loan of which we obtained from the sappers and miners.

I had at this time for a comrade, a Sergeant Burton, belonging to the same company, and we were attached to each other from the circumstance that we were both Cockneys. He and I had contrived to form a cave, just large enough to hold us, and we thought, with a little straw, and our blankets and greatcoats, we might contrive to pass the night without being frozen. Sergeant Burton was not at all soldierlike in his appearance, being on the wrong side of fifty, and having served some years on board a man-of-war; afterwards he joined the Tower Hamlets Militia and from them he volunteered into our regiment. He was one of those active, devil-may-care, rough-and-ready sort of fellows, that an officer would select if he wanted a job done off-hand, without any bother. Now, while he was taking home the implements we had borrowed, one of the largest sized shells, from the enemy's battery, burst in the air, immediately over us, and literally descended among us as a shower of iron. A large portion of the shell fell directly on the top of our cave, and destroyed in one moment the work of an hour. On Burton's return, he swore bitterly at the destruction of our work, and said to me, with the utmost seriousness, 'D——n it, Tom, how came you to let them do that!' As we could not again obtain the loan of the tools, we were obliged to walk or run about the whole night to keep the blood in circulation.

As soon as daylight appeared, the firing from the town forced us again to lie down. One of the officers, who was looking through the breastwork watching the enemy's batteries, suddenly drew himself down, observing, that a gun was just fired, the shot from which would come very close to us; the observation caused a young man, reclining next the officer, to raise himself up to look, and immediately his head was taken off.

Hitherto, we had been sheltered from the batteries, but this morning they took us in flank, opening on us some long forty-two pounders, from Fort Ferdinand; and against these shots we had no sort of shelter. About midday, we were relieved from this very dangerous position, where we lost a great many men, and retired beyond the village, but not out of the reach of the shot; one among other proofs we had of this, was, that a number of us were sitting round a fire, over which was a camp-kettle, containing our allowance of meat, when the pot was struck by a cannon-shot, and shattered to pieces, and some of those sitting round were very seriously injured.

During the next day, the enemy's fire was continuous, but ours rather languid, and as night set in, we commenced moving the guns and mortars from their position; and before daybreak, we were in full retreat from the place. The author of the history of the war has attempted to account for this sudden retreat, by stating, that Sir Thomas Graham was ordered to join [*the Prussian General von*] Bülow in some operation in another quarter: but the fallacy of this excuse will at once appear, from the circumstance of our taking up the position we previously occupied. The fact is, we were compelled to retire, absolutely for the want of ammunition for the artillery.

We lost, about this time, a fine young fellow through the dread of the lash. He belonged to the light company, and was so remarkably clean and well conducted, that he was generally selected at guard mounting, as orderly to the commanding officer, which not only saved him from the fatiguing duty of standing sentry, but was considered as a recommendation for promotion. For some slight crime, he was confined and tried by a court martial, and sentenced to receive three hundred lashes. When the morning of punishment came, he contrived, unseen by the guard, to take one of the firelocks from the rack, (they were all loaded) and placing the muzzle to his head, and putting his toe in the loop of a string, which he had fastened to the trigger, he blew his own brains out. Poor fellow! he was much esteemed by his comrades, and I think, on the whole, they were not sorry that he had thus freed himself from the horrors of the lash.

IV

Now are our brows crowned with victorious wreaths,
Our bruised arms hung up for monuments.

After the retreat from Antwerp, our brigade occupied a village called Putte, on the road and exactly half-way between Antwerp and Bergen-op-Zoom, and about three miles from the river Scheldt; having obtained possession of Fort Frederick Henry, a fort on the banks of the river, two miles from fort Lillo, then occupied by the French, and being on the same bank.

As there was no accommodation whatever for the lodging of troops at this place, the regiments of our brigade relieved each other in the occupation of it. It was of the utmost importance, as it completed our line of entrenchment, and enabled us most effectually to cut off all supplies to Bergen-op-Zoom, either from the country, or from Antwerp, by the river.

On 28 February, it being our turn to take the duty of this fort, we arrived there about ten o'clock in the forenoon, and relieved the 30th regiment. At this time a French line-of-battle ship, with a number of gun-boats, having dropped down with the tide from Antwerp, anchored just above the fort, and immediately opened their fire on us. The 30th, in going away was exposed to considerable danger, from the cannon balls which were flying about. One of these shots struck two men of the 30th, as they were crossing the bridge, taking off both legs from one of them, and one from the other.

Being now placed as a sentinel, on the bank of the river, between the two forts, I was immediately opposite the French man-of-war, and my instructions were, to lie down on the bank, that I might be less exposed to their shot, to keep a sharp look out upon them, and to give notice if I saw them attempting to land any men. The gun-boats kept rather behind the man-of-war, out of the range of the long forty-two-pounders at our fort. I could see everything that was passing on board the large ship, who, though she had fired a few broadsides at the fort, was now evidently making arrangements to bring as many of her guns as possible to bear on the fort, her object being to force a passage by, to relieve Bergen-op-Zoom. The bank of the river is about twenty feet above the surrounding country, and it is by cutting through this bank, that they can, to impede the operations of an enemy, inundate the country. Under this bank our regiment were tolerably secure from the enemy's shot, except when they had to assist the artillery-men in superintending the furnaces, and getting the red-hot shot ready for them.

As soon as the enemy had got everything ready, she opened upon us in right earnest; broadside after broadside was fired in the most rapid succession. It was the most awful sight I have ever been called on to witness. The whole of her shot passed obliquely by me, but appeared to make but little impression on the fort. The gun-boats, who could not reach the fort, amused themselves by firing at us poor fellows on the bank; but, as we were lying down, they did not hit any of us, though many of the shot passed very close. One, a nine-pounder, struck the bank within a yard of where I was reclining; I got it out of the bank, and afterwards took it to the fort with me. The enemy continued her fire for the space of four hours.

When we had been on our dangerous duty two hours, we expected to be relieved; but were disappointed, as to relieve us they would have had to bring the men on the top of the bank, where they would have been exposed to certain destruction. So we had to stand fast, and I was not sorry for it afterwards, as it gave me an opportunity of seeing the close of this affair.

At about three o'clock two men belonging to the Rocket Brigade arrived at the fort, and immediately commenced operations. The first rocket fell just astern of the enemy: the next one was sent with greater precision, and fell on the deck about midships. The greatest confusion prevailed on board, and they were shouting and running in all directions: of course, they expected some more to follow, and they were so evidently afraid of them, that they took advantage of the flood tide, slipped their cables, and made the best of their way back towards Antwerp.

We were now relieved, and on reaching the fort found it had suffered very considerably. None of the guns had been dismounted, and the casualties among the men, were two artillery men killed, five or six wounded, and a few of our men wounded by the splinters and stones which were scattered about. The fields behind the fort presented a very singular appearance, the hundreds of cannon balls which had fallen there, had ploughed up the earth in the most extraordinary manner.

As soon as we were rid of the enemy, some of the inhabitants of the neighbouring town of Sandvliet, came with a quantity of schnaps as a present to us; and a great number of the foolish fellows drank to such an excess, as to be quite unfit for duty. I had the credit of being a sober man, and this circumstance has on more than one occasion entailed on me additional duty. Such was now the case: although I had been on sentry six hours during the day, at ten o'clock at night I was obliged to go on again. My post, this time, was just outside the battery, and my duty was to give the alarm if any of the gun-boats should attempt to pass or land their men.

The night set in very dark, with a dense fog, and the only companion I had was one of the dead artillery men. He had been killed in the act of sponging his gun, and the ball that struck him, took his hand off at the wrist and forced it completely through his body. He had been laid outside the fort, with the intention of burying him next morning. I had to remain in this situation until two o'clock in the morning, before they could get men sober enough to succeed us.

Next day we were marched back to our quarters at Putte, and the third morning afterwards we were called out on a punishment parade; were taken to a secluded spot some distance from the village; a square was formed, the triangle erected, and the proceedings of the court martial which had been held, having been read over, eight men were tied up in succession and received two hundred lashes each: one hundred each short of their sentences. The colonel was highly exasperated, and threatened (for the future) to give the full punishment awarded to such men as should be found drunk on duty.

The next time it came to our turn for duty at the fort, a curious circumstance occurred, which one of the party had to remember as long as he lived. The bank to which I have already alluded, ran from our fort to Fort Lillo, a strong place occupied by the French. Close to our fort some strong defences were raised, and about a mile along the bank where I was posted during the attack on the fort. About half a mile further on was the post of our advanced sentinels, protected by some strong chevaux-de-frise, and not far from this, within hearing, were the advanced sentinels from the French fort. Our advanced sentinels this morning were two of the 95th Rifles, and they were visited by one of our captains, who, from his eccentricity, was called the 'mad captain'. As he could speak French fluently, he took it into his head that he could prevail on the French sentries to abandon their post, and come over to us. In order to make the experiment he advanced without his sword, inviting the Frenchmen to a parley. One of them did lay down his musket, and came slowly towards the captain. Suddenly, however, he drew back, took up his piece, took deliberate aim at the captain, and fired. Finding his ball had not taken effect, he placed the butt of his musket on the ground, holding it with the left hand by the muzzle, and, turning himself round, placed his right-hand on a certain part of his person.

Now, it so happened, that our two advanced sentries, the riflemen, were reclining on their breastwork, looking on; and one of them had the butt of his rifle at his shoulder, the muzzle resting on the chevaux-de-frise, and his finger on the trigger; and no sooner had the Frenchman placed his hand in the manner I have stated, than both the hand and the part of the person on which it was placed, were perforated by the rifleman's bullet. The fellow bounded about a yard in the air, fell heavily to the ground, and was carried away.

We were gratified, on this occasion, by a visit of a boat's crew from one of our men-of-war, lying down the river, towards Flushing. They brought some despatches from the Admiral, for General Graham. In their passage up, they had to pass several forts, which fired a few shots, but without effect. Though they had to repass the same forts, that circumstance did not appear to give them any uneasiness. This was our last visit to this fort.

A few days afterwards, our brigade went about ten miles, and were employed in throwing up some fresh entrenchments, under the super-intendence of the sappers and miners. While so engaged, we were very suddenly called away, and we were soon joined by Sir Thomas Graham. The information was given us, that we were going to storm the strong fortress of Bergen-op-Zoom; but when we had arrived within eight miles of that place, an aide-de-camp brought the disastrous intelligence, that the general who had been left with the troops before the town, and whose instructions were to watch the place, until Sir Thomas arrived to his assistance with the light brigade, had most imprudently made an attack.

However, possession was gained of the rampart; where, for want of order, they piled arms, and some of the men went into the houses and got drunk. The consequence was that when daylight appeared the French garrison were at their posts, and the British, who had

entered, were taken prisoners. A considerable number of them however, made their escape, and the rest were forced into the church,
and two pieces of cannon pointed at the entrance.

That this precipitately conducted affair took place contrary to
orders, was evident, from the chagrin Sir Thomas exhibited when
informed of it. Perhaps, had the generals survived we should have
heard something more of the matter, but as they fell, it was hushed up.

The French governor, having already more mouths than he could
find bread for, owing to our having for several months, cut off all
his supplies, was glad to dismiss the prisoners, on condition that they
should not serve in that country again during the war.

One of the regiments engaged in this affair was the 91st, composed
entirely of boys, so young, that they carried fusils instead of muskets;
and yet, these were the troops whom Generals Gore and Skerrit
thought proper to lead against the veterans of Napoleon! Had they
waited our arrival, there would have been no doubt of success.

By reference to the history of this period, it will be found that the
French were driven in upon all points. Wellington was advancing
with his victorious troops towards France. The Austrians, Russians,
Prussians, and Germans, who had continued the pursuit of the French
troops from Leipsic, were now in the environs of Paris; and nothing
remained for the French nation, but an unconditional surrender to the
Allies; which led to the deposition and banishment of the Emperor,
and the restoration of the former dynasty.

Lewis the Eighteenth having been seated on the throne of his
ancestors, by the Allied Sovereigns, the necessary orders were sent to
the commanders of garrisons, held by the French, to evacuate them,
and return to France. By virtue of these arrangements, the gates of
Antwerp were opened to us on 5 May, and we entered amidst the
acclamations of the people. We obtained possession of the citadel;
and the French left the same day, on their road for France. Such of
our troops as could not be accommodated in barracks, were billeted
on the inhabitants. Our regiment, with the 56th, was placed in the
barrack called the Cusern [*Caserne*] de Facons; and though the French
had left the rooms in rather a filthy state, we found them far prefer-
able to the accommodation we had been accustomed to the last five
months.

V The city of Antwerp was formerly one of the richest in Europe;
and is still a noble place. It is eight miles in circumference; and is
compared to a bow, the string thereof being represented by the river

Scheldt. Its walls are strong and beautiful, one hundred and ten feet broad, and on the top are a number of trees, regularly planted in rows. Along the walls are a number of bastions, contrived with great skill. There are thirteen gates; and the streets leading to them are straight and large; the buildings are many of them exceedingly grand, and the cathedral is the finest I have ever seen. There are about a dozen other churches, and a number of religious houses. The citadel is about a mile in compass; it is a pentagon, with some noble bastions, and commands both the city and the surrounding country.

Antwerp has been much celebrated in former days, for its extent of trade, its riches, and the magnificence of its buildings. It is stated that one of its citizens, named John Daens, having lent the Emperor Charles the Fifth, a million of gold, invited him to dinner; when, after a royal entertainment, he threw the Emperor's bond into a fire made of cinnamon.

Antwerp will always command a trade, on account of its noble river, which brings ships of large burthen up to the very shore.

As soon as we were fairly settled, it was a matter of curiosity with us to visit the village of Merxem, whence we had driven the enemy on 2 February; and although the time was so short, the alteration was astonishing. Many of the houses, which had only been partially destroyed, were again inhabited by their former tenants, and most of those which had been entirely destroyed, had been rebuilt. The family, whom I had the good fortune to rescue from a living tomb, were again in possession of their premises. They immediately recognised me, and manifested much joy at the meeting, making me promise to call very often to see them, and I certainly intended to visit them again; but, though we lay four months in Antwerp, I never had an opportunity of again going out that road.

Our duty in Antwerp was rather hard, mounting guard every third day, and on picket one night between; and I am sorry to say, that punishment-parades now were very frequent. I have often heard the observation made on service, 'that war was peace, and peace was war'; and the meaning of the paradox is, that in a state of actual war, the officers having to share all dangers and privations in common with the men, are induced to manifest a greater degree of kindness towards them; but as soon as hostilities cease, harassing parades, long drills, and corporal punishments are sure to increase. Such was now the case; and the average amount of punishment for slight offences, was three hundred lashes.

It is an extraordinary fact, that, horrible as this mode of punishment is, it seems to have no effect whatever, in reforming the character:—it invariably makes a tolerably good man bad, and a bad man infinitely worse. Once flog a man, and you degrade him for ever, in his own mind; and thus take from him every possible incentive to good conduct. Besides these regular modes of punishment, provost guards were established, who possessed and exercised the most arbitrary power.

A sergeant of our brigade was appointed provost-marshal for the district we were in, and in perambulating the streets at night, with a file or two of men, and a drummer, if he caught any of the men out after hours, he would either tie them to a lamp-post, and give them a dozen or two, or take them prisoners to his guard-room, and punish them there. He became at last so inflated with his own consequence, that late one night, when the main-guard fell in for inspection by the field officer, notwithstanding the said officer was his own colonel, he had the temerity to charge him with being drunk.

The colonel had been dining with the mess of his regiment, and there was no doubt a great deal of truth in the remark; but the truth must not always be spoken, especially against superiors—which the sergeant afterwards discovered to his cost. The colonel having retired, the sergeant took down the names of the guard, and asking them if the colonel was not drunk, they all replied that he was. Next day, the sergeant included, in his daily report, a charge against his colonel, of being drunk on duty; and the consequence was, that a general court martial was held, to try the colonel. The sergeant summoned the whole of the guard; and after making his own statement, called on them to support it: but as they were respectively produced (whether it was through hatred to the sergeant for his severity of conduct, as provost marshal, or fear of the consequences to themselves) not one of them could be induced to say the colonel was drunk. On the contrary, they stated on their oath, that they did not perceive any appearance of intoxication about him. The charge, therefore, having been so signally disproved by the accuser's own witnesses, the officer was honourably acquitted. The sergeant was then confined, and another general court martial held, before which he was found guilty of bringing a false charge against his commanding officer, when he was sentenced to be reduced to the ranks, to receive five hundred lashes, and to suffer six months solitary confinement. As far as his reduction to the ranks, and the infliction of the stripes, the sentence was carried fully into effect:

45

but death released the poor wretch from his solitary confinement.

Disgusting as this subject must be, to all persons having in their composition any portion of the 'milk of human kindness', yet I cannot forbear mentioning the following:—

I mounted guard one day at Fort Ferdinand, a strong place near Antwerp, mounting guns of very heavy calibre, not only commanding the river, but also the country north of Antwerp to a very considerable extent, (it was the guns of this fort which flanked us in our entrenchments while we were bombarding the town in February). During the afternoon I was on the rampart, and noticed the entrance of two officers on horseback. The guard saluted them and they rode round the ramparts. One of the sentinels (a very quiet steady man, who, from the darkness of his complexion, had been nicknamed the 'Black Prince') overcome by the oppressive heat of the sun had fallen asleep, and his musket had fallen from his hand against the cannon on which he was reclining. The officers, who now rode up to him, were Brigadier-General Crawford and his aide-de-camp, the former a strict disciplinarian, an Irishman, and an Orangeman. He had obtained an infamous notoriety in his own country, by his uncompromising and sanguinary conduct towards his unfortunate countrymen, during the rebellion in Ireland. He was only a militia officer there, and attained the rank of general as a reward for his *valuable services*. He was transferred to the regulars; was appointed captain in our regiment, and Brigadier-General of the army. The consequence of this was, that, when our regiment lay by itself, he fell in and did duty as captain of a company only; but if there were other regiments with us, then, by virtue of his brevet rank, he took command of the whole until some superior general officer should be present. Such was the officer who now rode up to the sleeping sentinel. He dismounted, took possession of the man's firelock, then called for the sergeant of the guard, and ordered him to confine the poor fellow, who was afterwards tried by a court martial, and sentenced to receive three hundred lashes.

There being very much sickness among us, we were for a while quartered on the suburban villages for the benefit of the air, where the time passed pleasantly enough, the inhabitants invariably treating us with the utmost kindness. For three weeks I was billeted, with sixteen other of our men, at the country-house of one of the richest citizens of Antwerp. He was not there, but sent very liberal instructions to his steward concerning us. The furniture, paintings and decorations of this mansion, were of the most splendid description. Though the people, on whom we were quartered were not of necessity compelled or expected to support us, as we had our daily rations, yet the old steward, willingly acting on his instructions, provided every day for us, and seemed offended if we did not make ourselves welcome.

The weather (July) being extremely fine, the long table for breakfast was spread under an avenue of trees at the back of the house; and this meal consisted of an abundance of new milk, white bread, eggs and coffee; and after the morning parade, such of us as were not for duty, were permitted to stroll through the extensive and delightful gardens and grounds, with full permission to partake of the fruit, of which there was a great redundancy. The only restriction imposed on us was, not to injure or destroy the trees or grounds; and so satisfactory to the steward, was our conduct in this respect, that on our leaving he not only gave us a certificate of good conduct, but gave us also a general invitation to call on him whenever we had the opportunity. Indeed, the kindness of this worthy man towards us, was most strikingly evinced on his receiving the news of the battle of Waterloo. Having taken our names down, he made enquiries after the battle respecting us, and manifested much sorrow on learning that nearly all were either killed or wounded. If I had had the opportunity afterwards, I think nothing would have afforded me greater gratification than to have paid a visit to this kind-hearted old gentleman.

During the stay in Antwerp, I was in the habit every Sunday, if off duty, of attending the cathedral, and though not of their religion, I could always admire the magnificence of the building and paintings, the splendid music and imposing ceremonies. At this time a most serious charge was laid against the principal of that establishment, to the effect that he had been for some time carrying on an intrigue with a nun. It was thought he did not succeed in establishing his innocence of the charge; but to prevent imputations of a like nature for the future, he had the courage to submit to an extraordinary and dangerous surgical operation.

While here I had the opportunity of residing, a little time, in the interior of a nunnery, which had been converted into a hospital, the nuns having been previously removed. I was confined here by a fever, the effects of a severe cold, and when I became convalescent I used to stroll through the extensive ground, consisting of a variety of delightfully laid out but secluded walks, each one terminating at the shrine of some particular saint.

A circumstance took place here one night, which might, rather unexpectedly, have terminated my career. There were about twenty of us in one sleeping apartment, each man's accoutrements hanging at the head of his bed; next to me lay a grenadier, a very powerful man, suffering much pain from a wound in the thigh. To compose him to sleep the doctor had given him a large dose of opium, which, instead of having the desired effect, conjured up to his imagination a thousand demons, whom he followed with his eyes round the room until they rested on my bed, when he raised himself up in bed, drew his bayonet, and by a violent effort threw himself across towards me, striking his weapon to the very socket into my bed, exultingly exclaiming, 'I have him now!' Fortunately for me I had been watching his movements, and springing from bed with the utmost alacrity, I pinned him by the arms and called for assistance, which was quickly rendered by the guard, and a sentry was placed over him for the rest of the night. The poor fellow slept afterwards for several hours, but appeared as if troubled by frightful dreams. Next morning he had no distinct recollection of anything that had passed; but as I was not altogether pleased with my position near him, I reported myself fit for duty, and left before the evening.

V

The cold shade of the aristocracy!

Antwerp participated largely in the general joy and rejoicing at the successful termination of the war, and the prospect of a lasting peace, under the guarantee of the Allied Sovereigns. The newspapers from England, at this time, teemed with the most glowing statements of the enthusiasm of all classes of people, and of the numerous and splendid fêtes given by the Prince Regent, in honour of his illustrious visitors. If any one had then predicted the astounding events which followed within a few months, he would have been deemed either a fool or a madman.

The great Napoleon had in the meantime, been consigned to the island of Elba, the place allotted for his future residence; and where, with the allowance it was stipulated he should receive, he would still be able to play the sovereign on a small scale. His separation from his old and faithful Guard—which has formed the subject of an excellent painting—was thus described, at the time, in a French paper.

'To the officers of the Old Guard, who were still with him, he spoke in nearly the following words—

"My dear friends and comrades, I bid you farewell. During the twenty years that we have acted together, I have been satisfied with you. I have always found you in the path of glory. All the powers of Europe have armed against me. A part of my generals have betrayed their duty: France itself has betrayed it. With your assistance, and that of the brave men who remained faithful to me, I have, for three years preserved France from civil wars. Be faithful to the new king, whom France has chosen. Be obedient to your commanders; and do not abandon your dear country, which has suffered too long. Pity not my fate: I shall be happy when I know that you are so likewise. I might have died; nothing would have been more easy to me, but I still wish to pursue the path of glory! What we have done, I will write. I cannot embrace you all; but I will embrace your general.

49

Come, General; let the Eagle be brought to me, that I may also embrace it. Ah! dear Eagle; may the kisses which I bestow on you, resound to posterity. Adieu, my children! Adieu, my brave companions! Once more encompass me." The staff, accompanied by the commissioners of the four Allied Powers, formed a circle round him; and Buonaparte got into his carriage, manifestly affected by the scene, dropping some tears.'

History furnishes but few instances of such entire devotion and enthusiasm, as was exhibited by the French soldiers towards their darling leader; even the dreadful reverses to which they were subjected, on their disastrous retreat from Russia, were not sufficient to wean their affections from the Emperor: they were still willing to fight for him—to die for him. One of the old French guard was dangerously wounded, and attended by an English surgeon; who, while probing for the ball, endeavoured to elicit from the man an acknowledgement that he was tired of his general. 'No, no,' said the veteran, 'cut on—cut deeper yet; and still you'll find the Emperor!' If we seek a reason for such extraordinary attachment, we shall find it in that constant attention of Napoleon, to the wants and wishes of his men; his identity with them in all their dangers; his prompt, profuse, but impartial distribution of rewards; his throwing open to the meanest soldier, the road of promotion to the highest honours; so that every man had a strong incentive to good conduct. When officers were killed or disabled, the vacancies were filled up from among the men who had been serving, who could sympathise with their comrades, in their dangers and privations; and while they had no difficulty in maintaining their authority, their conduct towards the men was kind and affectionate. No man, however elevated in rank or connexion, had any chance of promotion, but by passing through the various grades, commencing with the lowest.

But how different the practice in the British army!—where, as soon as vacancies occur in a regiment, they are filled up frequently by mere boys, just from school; who, though they may have acquired some theoretical knowledge of the art of war, know nothing of its practise; and who, knowing nothing of the fatigues and hardships the men have undergone, have no kindly feeling towards them.

When I joined the army, I was foolish enough to imagine that by good steady conduct, or by some daring act of bravery, I should be fortunate enough to gain a commission; but I very soon discovered the fallacy of this expectation. I certainly have known two or three instances in which commissions have been bestowed as the reward of merit; but such cases are 'like angel's visits, few and far between'. Indeed, according to the present constitution of our army, to obtain a commission places the individual in a worse position, especially in what are termed the 'crack regiments'; the aristocratic officers of which, send every man to 'Coventry', who cannot, like themselves, boast gentle blood, and whose private purse is not sufficiently well filled to support all the luxuries and extravagance of the mess table. Besides, how is it possible, supposing a deserving non-commissioned officer is promoted to a commission in such regiments as the 10th or 11th Hussars, that he can provide his equipments, which, I believe, under the most economical arrangement, amount to upwards of five hundred pounds.

The man who obtains a commission by merit in the British army, is placed in a most unpleasant and unenviable position. It was reported, that the Duke of York gave a commission to a deserving sergeant of the Guards, who waited on him afterwards, requesting to be unmade, describing the manner in which he was slighted by his brother officers, who positively refused to associate with him. The Duke told him to go back and take no notice, but he would try to alter the case. The colonel received orders to have the regiment ready, on a day named, for the Duke's inspection. The day came; the regiment fell in; the Duke arrived and inspected them, and afterwards, as they were standing at ease, the Duke called out the new-made officer and walked arm-and-arm with him, in front of the parade, for at least half an hour, the other officers looking on with the utmost astonishment. After the Duke's departure, the ex-sergeant found a marked difference in the conduct of his brother officers towards him, and for the future they were very anxious to cultivate the acquaintance of an officer, who appeared to be such an especial favourite with the Duke.

Taking all these things into consideration, I asked what incentive to good conduct is there in British service? The chances of a man obtaining a commission are about one hundred thousand to one against him; and the only benefits he is likely to obtain, is an admittance to Chelsea Hospital, or a pension of one or two shillings a day, if disabled in the service:—to be taken from him, however, if he should exercise the rights of a citizen, and take part in any public ebullition of feeling against the ministry of the day.

As the old song has it—

You may fight till you die, do the best that you can,
And the captain will reward you, with 'There lies a
   brave man!'

Should this country again be involved in war, it is to be hoped
the army will be placed on a different footing to what it has been,
and that commissions will not be bestowed on individuals, simply
because they belong to this or that noble family; but that they will be
given as the reward of merit. Then we may expect to have an efficient
set of officers; for while I admit that I have known many brave and
well-disciplined officers in the service, yet, on the whole I considered
them the most inefficient of any officers in the European armies.
If it were not for the ability and efficiency of their covering sergeants,
they would be very frequently at fault, and very often, when regiments or companies are ordered extra drill, for apparent blunders,
the fault really rests with some of the officers.

When doing duty with the Prussians, I have mounted guard with
a young nobleman, sustaining no higher rank than myself, and receiving no favours from his superiors on account of his fortuitous advantages of birth or connexion; obliged to take his turn of duty,
and any dereliction of that duty punished, as certainly with him as
with the meanest of his comrades. Contrast with this the haughty
conduct of many British officers, who fancy themselves made of
different stuff to the men, and consider it derogatory to their characters,
to use any other words towards them than those of command or abuse.
I have known however, many exceptions to these remarks.

The colonel of my own regiment, the present Lord Harris, always
considered himself the father of his regiment, and behaved towards
the men with the utmost kindness; and though he ordered and superintended a great number of corporal punishments, yet I verily believe
that nothing but an imperative sense of duty urged him to it; and he
always appeared to suffer as much mental anguish as the prisoners did
bodily suffering. No sooner was the probable efficiency of other less
disgraceful modes of punishment suggested to him, than he immediately adopted them. Where men have officers who treat them
kindly, they perform their duty with cheerfulness and alacrity; and
there is no service so desperate that they will not volunteer to perform
for officers whom they respect. To show the difference in the conduct
of the men, towards good and bad officers, I will mention a circumstance, which I witnessed in going through Germany.

We had been several days without any other provision than fruit, and one of the men was roasting potatoes by the camp-fire, when an officer came up, who was very generally disliked, and from the cadaverous colour of his complexion, was called the 'Sick Black'. Coming up to the fire, and assuming, for the moment, a look of the utmost kindness, he said, 'Smith, I wish you would give me a few of those potatoes?' 'I'll see you d——d first', was Smith's reply; (before giving it, however, he ascertained there was no one by that was likely to bear witness, in case the officer should charge him with disrespect). Another officer came up directly, Ensign [*Robert*] Stewart, and not knowing what had passed, he said to Smith, 'Jack, I wish you would sell me some of those potatoes.' 'No', said Smith; 'I will not sell you any—but I will give you as many as you like, on one condition:—that you will not give any to MacBean.'[1]

As an instance of the effects of kindness in reforming the character, I will relate the following:—When the regiment lay in the Tower, there was a fine young fellow in the Grenadiers who gave way to intemperate and disorderly conduct; was continually in the guard room, and at punishment drills; at length, he got drunk one night and deserted; was taken, and brought back a prisoner. The colonel sent for him, to his own room, having a great regard for him, and pointed out the consequences of his present course of life, promising to forgive him the crime of desertion (for which he had expected five hundred lashes) and to promote him, if he would only conduct himself well. The man, overcome with the kindness the colonel evinced towards him, promised amendment; and he kept his promise, for from that time, he became one of the soberest and cleanest men in the regiment; was promoted to the rank of corporal, then sergeant, then colour-sergeant; and when the sergeant-major was killed at Waterloo, he was appointed to that situation. But for the colonel's extraordinary kindness towards him, he would have been flogged for desertion, and the chances are, that he would ever afterwards have been a drunken, dirty, disorderly, vagabond.

The Prince of Orange having arranged with the people of Holland, the basis of the new Constitution, which was of the most liberal description, and the reorganisation of the Dutch troops being completed, the garrisons and fortresses were given up to them; the British troops

---

[1] William MacBean: Ensign 1 April 1813; wounded at Waterloo.

retiring to Belgium. Our removal, in the first instance, was to the ancient and beautiful city of Ghent, formed on the banks of two rivers, the Scheldt and Leys [*Lys*], which run through, and divide it into twenty-six islands, which are joined together by upwards of a hundred bridges. The circumference, within the old walls, is about seven miles. This place has been much celebrated in history, for its magnificent buildings; those, which remain, bear abundant evidences of their former grandeur. The cathedral is a fine building; its architectural beauties have been much admired. There are, besides, some ten or twelve other churches, besides a number of religious houses, the inhabitants being principally Roman Catholics. The castle was formerly the palace of the reigning Prince; and contained three hundred chambers. There is a citadel, which would have been considered strong, before the art of war attained such perfection, as it now has done. The country round is so extremely prolific, as to require very little aid to bring forth the most abundant crops. We found a marked difference here, in the manners of the people. To us indeed they were civil; but they evidently were most attached to the French interest— which is not to be wondered at, considering its contiguity to France, and the vast numbers of French families who had settled there.

We remained here about three weeks; and were then moved on to Tourney [*Tournai*], and took up our quarters in the citadel. This town has been a place of very considerable strength; indeed, so recently as the year 1795, it stood a siege by the Allied Troops, under the Duke of York, who erected batteries, and fired some days on the town, but did not attempt to force it. On the advance of the French republican troops, the British were compelled to retire so suddenly, as to leave a number of their cannon behind them. Before we had been long here, numbers of our men were attacked by a disease of the eyes; the symptoms were an intolerable itching, in the evening; during the night inflammation would take place, and in the morning the eyes would be completely closed. Those attacked, were led away to darkened rooms, and the surgeon began to operate on them: and whether it was their ignorance of the nature of the disorder, or their bungling manner of applying the lancet, they managed to deprive some men of the use of both eyes, and others of one. The inhabitants, themselves, were generally attacked in the same way, in the autumn. It was supposed to arise from the effluvium of the stagnant water in the trench round the walls, which contained a vast deal of animal and vegetable putrid matter.

As soon as the men could be moved, we were placed in another part of the town. A portion of the Foot Guards were laying with us here, and some of their aristocratic officers, made the astounding discovery, that the uniform of our officers was exactly like theirs, with the exception of a slight difference in the colour of the facings—theirs being dark blue, and ours a dark green. Of course, such a circumstance, as that there should be no difference in dress between the Guards and a fighting regiment, could not be tolerated. A consultation was held by them, on the subject; and a communication forwarded to the commander-in-chief in England; who lost no time in taking a matter of so much importance into his most serious consideration. The next despatches contained an order for the officers of the 73rd to divest themselves of two slips of gold lace, from the skirt of their regimental jackets, to prevent, for the future, the possibility of their being mistaken for officers of the Guards!

In the month of October we left Tourney, and proceeded to Courtray, or Cortrick as it was formerly called. It was once a place of very considerable strength, being situated on the river Leys, and well defended, both by art and nature. When we were there, however, the defences were in such a state of dilapidation, that it was altogether untenable as a fortress: only our regiment was quartered there. The duty was not severe, having but three guards to find.

I believe the motive for quartering the British troops through the towns of Belgium, at this time, was to ensure the tranquillity of the people, until the annexation of Belgium to Holland should be carried into effect, as agreed on by the Allied Powers, in their settlement of the boundaries of the different states.

Belgium, of right, belonged to Austria; but that power readily agreed to its being joined to Holland, on their receiving an equivalent for it. In another quarter, the proclamation of the (now) King of Holland, in reference to the incorporation of the two countries, was very unpopular; so much so, that where we were, they could not prevail on any of the inhabitants to assist in the reading of it; and that duty had to be performed under a guard of British bayonets. It was easy then to predict, that the union of two countries, different in religion, language, customs and manners, would exist only as long as a foreign army should be there to enforce it.

During our residence in this town, in consequence of the prevalence of the small-pox, the men were all examined, and those who had not had the disorder, were inoculated for it.

An accident of a curious nature befell one of our sergeants here. He was out rather late at night, and running home, in turning sharply round the corner of the street, he came in contact with two of the gen-d'armes, or police who were carrying their firelocks slung over their shoulders, with the bayonets pointing out in front, and the sergeant's thigh came in contact with one of the bayonets, which entered the front of the thigh, passed along obliquely for about four inches, and came out beneath. The poor fellow was regularly transfixed: they had not the courage, for some time, to pull the weapon out. There was no blame to the police, in the matter, as the sergeant came so unexpectedly on them. It was considered one of the worst bayonet-wounds that could be: the man never got the better of it. Other incidents, of a more disgraceful nature, here force themselves on my memory, and I feel bound to relate them.

The cheapness of ardent spirits, genuine hollands, direct from the distillery, was sold in the chandlers' shops, the same as small beer used to be in England; the price of the spirit (retail) was only eight-pence per quart. The consequence was, we had a great deal of drunkenness and crime; and, as a matter of course, a great many punishment-parades, which took place on the Esplanade, or piece of ground near the citadel, overlooked by a number of respectable houses; and the frequency of our disgraceful flogging exhibitions, created much horror and disgust, that at length a remonstrance was presented to our commanding officer, on the subject. I shall relate one of the cases which took place here, as being of rather an extraordinary nature.

Two prisoners were brought out, and the proceedings of the court-martial read, their crime having been the same—drunkenness and insubordination, under very aggravated circumstances, which certainly merited severe punishment; though nothing, in my opinion, can justify the use of the lash. The first prisoner was a young man belonging to the Grenadiers; his sentence was eight hundred lashes, out of which he received five hundred. The other prisoner was a drummer, young, small, and weakly; he had been punished before, and his back was scarcely healed from the last infliction. The first few strokes of the cat, laid the back bare to the bone. Someone, from mistaken motives of kindness, had given the poor wretch, before he came out, a copious draught of hollands, the effect of which was not perceptible until he was tied up; and then it maddened him. Instead of wincing from the stripes, he abused the commanding officer, and sung a variety of scraps of songs. The major who commanded that morning was exasperated at the apparent levity of the prisoner, and abused the drum-major for not making the drummers do their duty more effectually; and for every stroke the drummer gave the poor wretch, he received one from the drum-major's cane, across his own shoulders. At length, the major suspended the punishment; selected one of the drummers; and formed what is called a 'Drum-head court-martial'. The drum-major swore the man could punish more effectually, if he chose. He was found guilty of refusing to do his duty; was tied up there and then, and received one hundred and fifty lashes. The other punishment was proceeded with: but the poor creature, the strength of the spirits having evaporated, was not able to bear any more; he fainted, and was carried to the hospital in a state of insensibility.[1]

After the protest of the inhabitants, other modes of punishment were adopted. Solitary confinement, for the more serious crimes, and extra-guards and punishment-drills for the common offences. Sometimes the man would have to mount guard, and stand sentry with a log of wood, fastened by a chain to his leg. Crime did certainly not prevail to the same extent afterwards, as it did before. Solitary confinement was more especially dreaded by the men.

With these exceptions, we passed the winter very comfortably in this place. I was billeted with eight or nine others, at a public-house called the 'Parrot'; in reference to the landlord of which, strange tales were told, and believed too. Being of an extremely jealous nature, it was reported that he had poisoned three of his wives. He had been subjected to two examinations; but no conclusive evidence having been adduced, he was released. He was now about seventy years of age, and his former cruelties did not prevent his getting another wife, who was then about thirty years old. Nor did the reported fate of his former wives, prevent the present one from forming a connexion with one of our sergeants; whose criminal intercourse with her was beyond a doubt.

In the early part of March 1815, we left this place, and lay three or four days at a village, about three miles distant. From thence we were taken on an excursion across the country, for a distance of thirty miles, through cross country-roads, and over fields, hedges and ditches. At night, dreadfully fatigued, we lodged in some barns, and early in

---

[1] The regiment was at this time under the command of Major Kelly, the Colonel being absent. [*T.M.*]

the morning fell in; the colonel having received orders to take the regiment back that night to the village we had left the day before. On our return we encountered a very severe storm, of wind, hail and rain; the men were so completely knocked up, and some of them literally knocked down, by the hailstones, or more properly speaking, masses of ice, that they were almost in a state of mutiny, at being so harassed without any object. The colonel was requested to halt the men at some place short of their destination; but he replied, 'he must go the whole distance with the colours, even if he did not take thirty men with him.' Numbers of the men were actually unable to proceed; and only about one hundred of us went in with the colonel and colours; and it was several days afterwards before we could muster the men.

I never could learn the reason for this extraordinary march. In war time, we were frequently called on to make forced marches, but then we knew there was a necessity for it, and an object to be gained; but here there was no apparent motive, beyond the mere caprice of the general.

While stopping here, for the first and last time in my life, I had my fortune told me, not only unsolicited, but under circumstances of a rather extraordinary nature. I was billeted by myself, on a cottage about a mile from the village; and the only inmates were an old man, his daughter, and her infant. The husband of the young woman was serving with the Belgian troops, and was then stationed at Ghent. The old man was dangerously ill, with the scarlet fever; and as they had no relatives near them, and the neighbours not liking to visit them under the circumstances, I occasionally assisted the young woman in ministering to her father's wants, for which she was extremely grateful. On one occasion, she hastily drew from the cupboard a pack of cards, and after turning them over in a variety of ways, she at length pronounced my fate; which was, that I should go in one more grand battle; that I should then go home to England, and marry a certain person, who was then waiting for me. I laughed at the prediction, at the time; but have often since wondered at its accuracy.

We left this place again very suddenly, and apparently on the same wild-goose-chase as before. After marching upwards of thirty miles, by a roundabout way, we reached the city of Tourney at one o'clock in the morning, dreadfully tired. The night was very dark; the street lamps were nearly all out; and as we were not expected, no billets had been provided; and cold as the night was, most of the men took out their greatcoats, and laid down on the pavement. An intimation was given us, that if we could prevail on the persons on whom we had billeted when we were last here, to open the door to us, we might do so; but we were strictly prohibited from making use of force or intimidation. As I had been on exceedingly good terms at my quarters, I thought I would try the experiment. Groping my way therefore, in the dark, I reached the place alone, just as the clock struck two, and rang at the bell. Presently the servant came, but not being thoroughly awake, I was some time in making her understand who I was; when I did do so, she uttered an exclamation of surprise; but went and acquainted her master and mistress of the circumstance, and by the time I was admitted, the whole establishment was up. Even the children came running round me, almost in a state of nudity. I was always kind to the children, and that sometimes made me a favourite with the parents. After the gratulations were over, I took some little refreshment, and went to my old bed, completely worn out with the day's journey. After breakfast, next morning, they insisted that I should not seek another billet, but come and live with them, without one; but I never saw them afterwards, as we left the town immediately.

We proceeded directly to Ath, another strongly fortified place, on the borders of France; where we obtained information of the return of Napoleon. Nothing was known as to his future movements; but it was considered most likely, that his first attempt would be to drive the British from Belgium, when the inhabitants and troops would no doubt join him.

VI

How quick the changes of the soldier's fame,
The bold, the vaunting Corsican will name;
He feels no pleasure but in war's alarms,
The trumpet's clangor, and the din of arms,
Cheering his partners of the tented field,
'Nor sheathe your swords! (he cries) till all shall yield.'

In 1815, while the main European powers were meeting at Vienna to settle the affairs of the continent, Napoleon escaped from Elba and established himself once more as the ruler of France. The Congress of Vienna would not accept this new situation even when Napoleon promised to pursue a peaceful policy for the future. They outlawed him and set in motion plans to re-constitute their armed forces and move them against him.

All this took time, and Napoleon decided to strike before the Allies could concentrate. In June only the British under Wellington and the Prussians under Blücher were in the field, and even their forces were widely scattered; the British in the neighbourhood of Brussels and the Prussians about Ligny.

Showing great strategic skill Napoleon moved north through Charleroi and surprised the Allies while they were still separated. His plan was to defeat the Prussians, to drive them off towards the east, and then to move north against the isolated forces of Wellington. Quatre Bras, the cross-roads where the main north-south road between Charleroi and Brussels met the road joining with Ligny, was the key point; and Ney's lack of success in taking it ruined his plans. Napoleon defeated the Prussians at Ligny, but instead of making off east the Prussian army retreated north to Wavre, not very far from Wellington's forces. This was the first thing that went wrong for Napoleon. Then Ney who was ordered to take the Quatre Bras cross-roads failed to do so owing to the stubbornness of the Allies' resistance there. Ney called back to help him d'Erlon's reserve corps which should have completed the rout of the Prussians; but d'Erlon did not reach Ney in time to be effective at Quatre Bras either. The Allied force at Quatre Bras having done its job well and foiled Napoleon's plans was then able to retreat in good

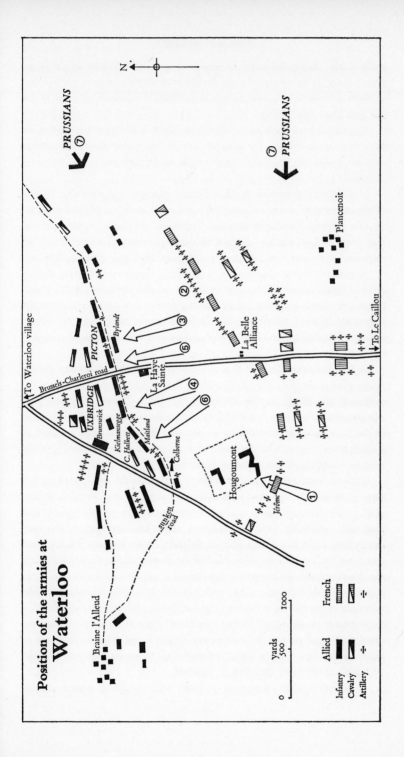

Position of the armies at

Waterloo

N

PRUSSIANS
⑦

PRUSSIANS
⑦

Plancenoit

To Waterloo village

PICTON

Bylandt

②

La Belle
Alliance

Brussels–Charleroi road

La Haye
Sainte

To Le Caillou

③

⑤

④

⑥

UXBRIDGE

Brunswick

Kielmansegge

C. Halkett

Maitland

Colborne

Hougoumont

Jérôme

sunken
road

Braine l'Alleud

yards
0   500   1000

Allied

French

Infantry

Cavalry

Artillery

order to the strong defensive position chosen by Wellington at La Haye Sainte, south of the village of Waterloo. Here on the ridge across the Charleroi —Brussels road Wellington, armed with Blücher's promise to come to his aid next day, stood at bay.

Sergeant Morris took part with his regiment in the encounter at Quatre Bras and in the retreat. He describes vividly the storm during the retreat and the unpleasant conditions of the night in the rain before the Battle of Waterloo.

Wellington's strength was about 85,000 men and 156 guns, but 17,000 of the troops were placed at Hal eight miles away on his right flank to guard against a French turning movement. Napoleon had about 72,000 men and 246 guns. Blücher had had 84,000 men at Ligny but was able to bring less than half that number to Wellington's aid, and then only by late afternoon.

Napoleon's battle plan for 18 June was a simple one: a great battery of eighty guns would line up just to the east of the Brussels-Charleroi road (2 on map) and by a fierce bombardment pave the way for an assault on the very centre of Wellington's position. D'Erlon's corps would enter the breach, and the Imperial Guard and eighty squadrons of cavalry would complete the rout.

In fact, however, the fight began by divisional bombardments and French infantry attacks on the flanks to draw away British reserves from the centre,(1) moreover the attack on the British right, under Jérôme Bonaparte, on Hougoumont was not only defeated by the stubborn resistance of the Guards in the farm, but was persisted in so long that it occupied large numbers of French troops throughout the battle and weakened other attacks elsewhere without occupying a corresponding number of British troops.

After the bombardment proper, d'Erlon's attack on the centre with 18,000 men in divisional columns (3) produced the first crisis of the day for the Allies. The French nearly achieved a break-through in spite of the fact that their unwieldy divisional columns made excellent targets, for they swept back Bylandt's Dutch-Belgian Brigade. Picton's troops behind, however, rose up, moved forward and halted the French. Before they could renew the assault, Lord Uxbridge's heavy brigades, consisting of the Household Cavalry, KDGs, Royals, Greys and Inniskillings, overwhelmed them. The Gordons supported their brothers the Greys by rushing forward clutching their stirrups to the cry of 'Scotland for ever!' Flushed with their success the cavalry charged on too far into enemy territory and were in turn cut to pieces so that only one in three remained to fight again. Nevertheless, the first crisis of the battle had been surmounted.

Waterloo is often pictured as a battle with hordes of French cavalry

*charging British redcoats in squares. The next phase (4) is when it happened.
Ney misinterpreted as a retreat the departure from the centre of some British
wounded, French prisoners and empty wagons, and sent in huge cavalry
charges—first of 5,000 men each and finally of 9,000 horsemen, largely
without infantry and artillery support—against troops still unshaken (4).
The British and Allied infantry in squares supported by artillery held all
these charges, and Sergeant Morris describes how his regiment dealt with the
French cavalry and how the Duke expressed himself perfectly satisfied with
the conduct of the 73rd before moving on to visit the Guards on the right.
The 73rd were in Major-General Sir Colin Halkett's brigade along with
the 30th, the 33rd, and the 69th. They can be seen next to Maitland's
Guards on the map.*

*What is usually considered as the real crisis of the battle came at about
six o'clock. Attacking at last with a force of all arms (5), Ney captured La
Haye Sainte and broke through the Allied centre. Now, however, the
Prussians were arriving in some numbers (7), and this enabled Wellington
to reinforce his centre from his left. Napoleon, when asked by Ney for the
vital reinforcements which could have brought them victory, replied, 'Troops!
Where do you expect me to get them? Do you expect me to make them?'
Later, however, when the time was less opportune Napoleon sent in his
Imperial Guard (6). The Guard was held by Maitland's 1st Foot Guards,
who were given the title of Grenadiers in recognition of their defeat of what
were thought at the time to be the grenadiers of the Imperial Guard. It was,
however, probably the chasseurs of the Imperial Guard and not the grenadiers
who attacked them. In fact many might claim to have repulsed the Guard, for
the French came up at a number of points along the Allied front. The 52nd
Light Infantry (now 1st Greenjackets) under Sir John Colborne can, however,
certainly claim to have played a decisive part. Coming forward and then
sweeping east, they struck the flank of the Imperial Guard. This finally
made the French retreat so that to the shout of 'La Garde recule!' there was
a wholesale withdrawal. The Young Guard valiantly held Plancenoit until
nightfall so preventing the Prussians from cutting Napoleon's line of retreat,
and three squares of the Old Guard resisted for a while to cover the Emperor's
departure. The rest of the French Army panicked and fled in disorder pursued
ruthlessly through the night by the Prussians.*

During the months of April and May, the British were leaving the
distant towns, and gradually concentrating as near as possible to the
Belgian frontiers. The most impenetrable mystery seemed to be
observed in reference to Napoleon's future movements: that he was

preparing for some daring enterprise, there was no doubt; but while waiting the development of his plans, we were placed in quarters, with such arrangements that the division could concentrate at a very short notice.

Our regiment, with the 30th second battalion (ours also was a second battalion, the first battalions of both regiments being at the time in the East Indies) were quartered on a sweet village, three miles from the town of Soignes; the latter place was the rallying point for the whole of our divisions.

Our situation here was pleasant in the extreme, as we had little duty to perform. I was quartered, with my comrade, on a miller, about a mile and a half from the village. The family consisted of the miller, his wife, and two daughters of the ages of sixteen and seventeen; and as we were both young men and tolerably good-looking, both the miller and his wife were rather shy of us at first, keeping the girls always away from us in the day time, and carefully locking them in their chamber at night; but as they became better acquainted with us, this reserve wore off, and they did not even object to the girls strolling with us through the meadows: nor had we any intention of abusing the confidence thus reposed in us. One of the girls was much attached to my comrade, and would not have needed much persuasion to become his wife.

In the beginning of June, my old friend Sergeant Burton was commissioned to go to the town of Soignes, to purchase some shoe-leather; his wife, who was about his own age, and as great an oddity as himself, would of course go with him, and he also requested me to accompany them. We selected the nearest road, across some fields, and reached the town about twelve o'clock, and after looking about us a little, we found a large currier's establishment, the proprietor of which invited us in, and exhibited his stock of leather, which I thought sufficiently large to provide shoes for the whole British army, for two or three years. Sergeant Burton, who (amongst his other professions) had been a shoemaker, and was therefore a judge of leather, after making a careful selection of such materials as he thought proper, had them all placed together. Mrs Burton, who carried the purse, paid for them (the amount was somewhere about ten or twelve pounds) and directions were given for them to be sent to the sergeant's quarters. Having settled the business matters, the proprietor, probably well-satisfied with the profits of the transaction, invited us into a small room, and provided some substantial refreshment; after which, some excellent hollands was produced, and our worthy host endeavoured to amuse us, by the relation of various anecdotes, referring to his former military service, in the republican army of France, in their excursions through Holland; but, as he could speak but little English and we knew very little French, we did not relish his French half so well as we did his hollands.

Time passed rapidly on, and the old gentleman perhaps began to think we had had enough, when he invited us to take coffee, which was very acceptable, especially to Mrs Burton, who though accustomed daily to take a *small* portion of her husband's allowance of spirits, exhibited unequivocal symptoms of having now taken a little drop too much; not that she would admit the fact, but attributed her slight indisposition to the heat of the weather. After disposing of the coffee, with a moderate quantity of bread and butter, we had one parting glass with our worthy friend the currier, and then started for home.

It was near nine o'clock, and we calculated it would take us, even by the shortest cut, at least an hour to reach the village, under the most favourable circumstances; but the sky was darkening rapidly, and exhibited strong symptoms of an approaching storm; and to make it worse, my companions began to quarrel, and I had much trouble to prevent them from proceeding to blows. During the squabble, we had unfortunately passed the turning by which we had come in the morning, and Burton insisted on going to an inn by the road-side, to take shelter from the rain, which was now coming down in right earnest.

We found in the house several Flemish travellers, who looked rather suspiciously on us, until the sergeant called for some hollands, and invited them to drink, which led to further remonstrance on the part of Mrs Burton, who, like myself, chose rather to battle with the storm than to be absent from our quarters without leave; as our pass only extended to nine o'clock in the evening. The sergeant, however, was obstinate, and 'would not stir for all the officers in the country'. His wife, at last, left the place by herself; and I was trying to prevail on him to follow: when, finding she was really gone, he hurried out in a state of great excitement; and, before I could overtake them, he had drawn his sword and inflicted a wound on her head, cutting through her bonnet and cap. As soon as I came up, I caught her, fainting, in my arms, and found the blood from the wound trickling down very fast. Burton was instantly sobered, and sorry for what he had done, he assisted me in conveying her back to the inn.

The landlord, the moment of our departure, had closed the doors, but he let us in, and brought some water. Having had some experience in such matters, I washed the wound, separated the hair from it, and bound it up with a portion of the sergeant's shirt, which I made him tear up for that purpose. As it was impossible (now) to think of going that night, the landlord, as he could not accommodate us with beds, provided us with two trusses of clean straw, and we laid down together; Burton and his wife soon fell asleep, but the probability of the wound bleeding afresh, kept me awake the great part of the night. Early in the morning we got up, had breakfast, and started home.

The sergeant was sadly chagrined at having struck his poor old woman, who had so long been the companion of his journeys, but they made the matter up, and we began to consider what excuse we should offer for our absence; at last, we agreed to trump up a story, that having been attacked in the fields, Mrs Burton receiving the blow intended for her husband, had caused the delay. We were not, however, under the necessity of relating this story, as our absence had not been noticed, and nothing further was said about the matter.

Although we were so pleasantly situated here, we began to get tired of the monotony, and there was a restlessness, and an anxiety to know what the French were about, and how soon our services would be required, as it was universally believed that Napoleon would make a desperate attempt to drive the Anglo-Prussian armies from Belgium, when, if successful, he would not only be at liberty to attack the other troops, as they should successively arrive, but his success would also be the means of inspiring his men with that enthusiasm, which was so necessary to ensure his ultimate success.

On 15 June, some of the officers and men were playing at ball, against the gable-end of a house in the village, when an orderly dragoon brought dispatches from General Halkett, who commanded a brigade, ordering us to fall in immediately, and proceed to the town of Soignes. The men were scattered about, variously engaged; but they soon understood, from the roll of the drums, and the tones of the bugles, that their attendance was immediately necessary, in marching order. About four o'clock, the order came, and by six we had fallen in, and were off. On our arrival at Soignes, we found the town filling fast with troops. There was evidently something extraordinary in this sudden movement, but no one knew the cause. About nine o'clock that night, we had one day's provision served out, and as the meat was raw, we thought it advisable to cook it, not knowing how we might be situated next day. At twelve o'clock at night, we fell in; and in another hour had left the town behind us, and soon entered what is very appropriately called, the 'dark wood of Soignes'.

Thy wood, dark Soignes, holds us now,
Where the tall beech's glossy bough,
    For many a league around,
With birch and darksome oak between,
Spreads deep and far a pathless screen,
    Of tangled forest ground:
Stems planted close by stems, defy
The advent'rous foot—the curious eye,
    For access seeks in vain,
And the brown tapestry of leaves,
Strewed on the blighted ground, receives
    Nor sun, nor air, nor rain.

Our superior officer had received some hasty and ill-defined instructions, to take us on this road; and as it was not known how near the enemy might be, it was necessary to throw out an advanced guard, and proceed with caution. The progress we made through the wood was so slow, that by eight o'clock in the morning we had not proceeded more than ten miles. We then halted for an hour, the general anxiously expecting some instructions of a more definite nature, but the other troops were in motion in the same direction: it was not until twelve o'clock that we were made acquainted with the service on which we were going.

On reaching the town of Nivells [*Nivelles*], we were informed of the advance of a large French army, commanded by Napoleon, and that they had been engaged with the Prussians, the day before, at Ligny; we passed through the town, and halted on an extensive common, and could then distinctly hear the sound of artillery. Some commissariat waggons coming up, we received three days' allowance of provisions, consisting of salt beef and ship's biscuit, it being impossible to provide, on the moment, fresh provision for so many.

We were now ordered to fall in and advance, and we soon heard the firing of musketry, as well as artillery. We were urged forward with the utmost celerity, and about three o'clock, entered the field of battle, at Quatre Bras, notwithstanding our fatigue, having marched about twenty-seven miles, exposed to a burning sun. Our brigade at this time, consisted of the 30th, 33rd, 69th and 73rd, commanded by Major-General Sir Colin Halkett. The ground, for a considerable distance, being covered with rye, and of an extraordinary height, some of it measuring seven feet, prevented us from seeing much of the enemy; but, though we could not see them, they were observing us. We continuing to advance, the glittering of the tops of our bayonets, guided towards us a large body of the enemy's cuirassiers, who, coming so unexpectedly upon us, threw us in the utmost confusion. Having no time to form a square, we were compelled to retire, or rather to run, to the wood through which we had advanced; and when we rallied, the 69th unfortunately lost their king's colours.

We were again led on to the charge, in conjunction with the 'Black Brunswickers', commanded by the Duke of Brunswick, and this time we were successful, and drove the enemy, against whom we were pitted, a considerable distance across the plain. In this charge we lost several officers and about thirty men. The brave officer [*Lieutenant John Acres*], whom I have before alluded to, on our attack on Merxem, here received a wound of which he soon afterwards died, lamented by all who knew him.

Not having any enemy immediately before us, at this particular time, we were ordered to lie down, to avoid the shots, which were flying thickly round us. The colonel ordered two companies out skirmishing; the light company, and the company to which I belonged, were detached on this duty, but not together. Our company was unfortunately commanded by a captain, sixty years of age; who had been upwards of thirty years in the service, but was never before in action. He knew nothing of field movements, and when going through the ordinary evolutions of a parade, the sergeant was obliged to tell him what to say and do. He now led us forward, and we fired a few shots at a portion of the enemy who were within reach. Presently we saw a regiment of cuirassiers making towards us, and he was then at his wits' end, and there is no doubt we should all have been sacrificed, had we not been seen by the adjutant of our regiment [*Ensign Patrick Hay*]—a fine spirited fellow, who had been our regimental surgeon, but through the interest of the colonel, exchanged to ensign and adjutant. On seeing us in this perilous position, he immediately rode up, and exclaimed, 'Captain Robinson,[1] what are you about? Are you going to murder your men?' He directly ordered us

1 Probably Captain Alexander Robertson.

to make the best of our way to the regiment, where we arrived just in time to form square; and on the cuirassiers coming up, and finding us so well prepared, they wheeled off to the left, receiving from us a volley as they retired. They then attacked the 42nd, by whom they were again repulsed, and compelled to retire.

We were no more actively employed; but had an opportunity of looking round, and could see the French troops retiring to the wood in their rear. By degrees, the fire slackened, and about eight o'clock ceased altogether, and the field of battle was left in our possession.

Though it is considered a sort of treason to speak against the Duke, yet, I cannot help making a few observations upon the extraordinary fact, that we had neither artillery nor cavalry in the field; there was a brigade of German artillery, and some few Brunswick horse. The reason given for the absence of our own cavalry and artillery, was, that they were quartered at too great a distance to be brought up in time. But, should it have been so? In cantonments, each division should have a portion of cavalry and artillery with them, so that they might, upon a small scale, be complete of themselves; and this arrangement would not at all prevent or impede the concentration of the whole. Fortunately for the Duke, the result was successful; had it been otherwise, he would have been deeply censured.

As soon as the firing ceased, we piled arms, and lay down among the dead and the dying. Among the occurrences of the day, I may mention the following:— On our entrance in the battle, we met a young man, a private of the 92nd regiment, whose arm had been taken off close to the shoulder, by a cannon ball. On passing us, he exclaimed, 'Go on, 73rd give them pepper! I've got my Chelsea commission!' Poor fellow! I should think, from the nature of his wound, he would bleed to death in half an hour, unless he obtained the most prompt and efficient surgical attendance, which he was not likely to do, as there were so many wounded waiting their turn to be attended to. I never was struck by a ball; but I have often noticed that those who are, do not always feel it at the time.

Ensign [*Thomas*] Deacon, of our regiment, was on my right, close to me, when we were charging the enemy, and a private on my left being killed by a musket-ball through the temple, the officer said, 'Who is that, Morris?' I replied, 'Sam Shortly'; and, pointing to the officer's arm, where a musket ball had passed through, taking with it a portion of the shirt-sleeve, I said, 'You are wounded, Sir.' 'God bless me! so I am,' said he, and dropping his sword, made the best of his way to the rear. After getting his wound dressed, he went in search of his wife, who, with her three children, he had left with the baggage guard. During the whole night, he sought her in vain; and the exertion he used was more than he could bear, and he was conveyed by the baggage-train to Brussels.

The poor wife, in the meantime, who had heard from some of the men that her husband was wounded, passed the whole night in searching for him among the wounded, as they passed. At length, she was informed that he had been conveyed to Brussels, and her chief anxiety then, was how to get there. Conveyances, there were none to be got; and she was in the last state of pregnancy; but, encouraged by the hope of finding her husband, she made the best of her way on foot, with her children, exposed to the violence of the terrific storm of thunder, lightning, and rain, which continued unabated, for about ten hours. Faint, exhausted, and wet to the skin, having no other clothes than a black silk dress, and light shawl, yet, she happily surmounted all these difficulties; reached Brussels on the morning of the 18th, and found her husband in very comfortable quarters, where she also was accommodated; and the next day gave birth to a fine girl, which was afterwards christened 'Waterloo Deacon'. He never joined us again, but went out with his family, to the first battalion, in the East Indies.[1]

On our last charge, the Duke of Brunswick was killed, at the head of his troops. He had been wounded twice before, but would not leave the field. Influenced by feelings of the most deadly hatred to the French, he had clothed his troops in black, with the skull and crossbones on their caps; and they were all sworn neither to give nor take quarter from the French. The Duke, and his men too, kept their oaths inviolate; they fought bravely, and suffered severely.

During the operations of the afternoon, we suffered much from thirst. There was a stream of water near the wood, in our rear, which would have been sufficient for us, but it was unfortunately rendered useless to the larger number, from the circumstance that a great many of the men who had been killed on its banks, had been thrust into it; this, however, did not prevent some of the men from filling their canteens with it, though tinged with human blood. In the evening we obtained a plentiful supply of pure water; and having sent out some pickets to prevent surprise, we sought that repose which we so much needed, after the excessive fatigue of such a long day.

[1] Deacon, then a half-pay Captain, was still alive in 1846.

I was awakened about midnight, and was sitting meditating on the occurrences of the past day, and thinking of the poor fellows we had lost, and wondering whose turn it would be on the morrow. The corn, which had covered the field in the day-time, was now all trodden down, and we had an uninterrupted view across the plain; and such a scene by moonlight, was grand but awful! Near me, was a group of our officers, with the colonel, who had formed a circle round an officer who had just arrived from England—Lieutenant Strahan.

On his arrival at Ostend, he learned there was a probability of an engagement, and, anxious to have a share in it, he had, by paying liberally, travelled post-haste, and joined us on the field of battle by moonlight, at midnight. He expressed his regret that he had not arrived earlier, to have shared in the glories of the fight. 'Oh!' said the colonel, 'if you are fond of such glory, you will have plenty of it tomorrow.' 'I hope so', was the reply. The officers drew their cloaks around them, and lay down to obtain some sleep, the newly-arrived lieutenant closing the conversation by observing, 'Good night, gentlemen: I hope those French fellows will not give us the slip before morning: I should feel greater disappointment at my delay, if I thought we should not have the opportunity of a brush with them tomorrow!'

Poor fellow! how little did he then suppose that even long before we should be engaged with the enemy, on the morrow, he would be in his grave; yet, such was the case.

About six o'clock, on the morning of the 17th, some of the outline sentinels began firing on each other. It was taken up by the pickets, and the whole line was soon in motion, and for a couple of hours were employed in cleaning their arms, and preparing for the renewal of the fight. Only a few of the enemy's advanced posts were to be seen. The main body, we were informed, had during the night been joined by Napoleon, in person, with a very large reinforcement. We also had been reinforced, and having now some cavalry and artillery, we assumed rather a formidable appearance, mustering probably about twenty thousand men.

Our first movement was to retire in line, and the word was given 'Right about face, march!' The muskets, instead of being shouldered as they generally are, were at the trail, that is, the middle of the firelock is grasped by the right hand, and carried horizontally, the muzzle in front; the officer [*Strachan*], who had so recently joined us was attached to our company. The men were surprised to see him, being most of them asleep when he arrived. He was in the rear before the line changed front, and instead of going to what then became the rear, he merely faced to the right-about, and marched on five or six paces in front of the line. The firelock of the man immediately behind him [*Jeremiah Bates*], going off, by accident, the ball entered the officer's back, and passed through his heart; the surgeon [*Duncan McDearmid*] examined, and immediately pronounced him dead. His purse, sword, and epaulettes, were taken care of, the loose earth was removed with swords, a rude grave was formed, the body was placed in it, covered over; and the line, which had halted when the accident took place, now resumed its march. He, who had travelled with such extraordinary haste in pursuit of honour and glory, died by the hand of one of his own men, and became the inhabitant of a solitary inglorious grave! Some little enquiry was made, and it appeared the accident had been caused by a portion of the corn, which had, here and there, resumed its upright position, had got entangled with the trigger, and caused the explosion.

By eleven o'clock, the army commenced its retreat to Waterloo. The reason, we supposed, at the time, was that the enemy had now too great a superiority in numbers, to give us any chance of success; our retiring therefore, to take up a fresh position, would give us the double advantages of effecting a junction with the whole of our forces, and being near to our supplies.

Some of the troops retired by the Brussels road, others to all roads to the right and left, as near as possible, on parallel lines of march. We were on the right of the main road, and were urged on with the utmost celerity, as there was no doubt the French would pursue us, as soon as they should discover our retreat.

The road we took was circuitous, and very fatiguing, having many steep hills to get up. About noon we halted at a small village, for half an hour's rest; and I had the good fortune to get my canteen filled with some malt liquor, which had been found in the cellar of a gentleman's house. That it might be got at with the greater facility, the heads of the barrels were driven in, and the liquor running about the floor, the men went in knee-deep and filled their canteens; and by this mode, a greater number were able to obtain a supply, than if they had waited to draw it off.

Having resumed our march, the sky suddenly darkened; and as we were going over a very high hill, we appeared to be enveloped in clouds, densely charged with the electric fluid. The rain descended literally in torrents. At no great distance, we heard the booming of artillery, and we judged the French advanced parties had overtaken our rear. Our journey hitherto had been up hills, and now we had some very steep hills to descend; and the rapidly accumulating water came down with such inconceivable force, that it was with the utmost difficulty we could keep our feet.

On emerging from this obscure road to the main road to Brussels, at the village of Genappe, the scene was grand, but of the most fearful description. On our right was the rear of our troops, on their way to Waterloo. On the hills, to the left, the main body of the French were rapidly advancing; in Genappe, was a body of the enemy's cuirassiers, whose advance the 7th British hussars vainly endeavoured to check, when the Earl of Uxbridge brought up the Oxford Blues and the Life Guards, and drove the cuirassiers back. I had an opportunity of witnessing the whole of this affair, as our regiment was in the rear, and I was compelled, at this time, to stop, to remove some gravel which had got into my boots.

The French flying artillery were close upon us, and their continual discharges, the cracking of the thunder, the vivid flashes of lightning, and the 'pelting of the pitiless storm', presented, altogether, a spectacle which few who witnessed will ever forget while living.

As soon as the troops reached that part of the Brussels road, nearest to the farm-house of La Haye-Sainte, the different brigades filed off to the right or left, to take up their respective positions; and it was now understood that this was to be our battlefield, if the enemy should think proper to engage us.

Our brigade was placed about midway between La Haye-Sainte and Hugamont [*Hougoumont*]; the Foot Guards were on our right; the whole of the ground was covered with corn, and the soil of so loose a nature, that, owing to the heavy rain, which continued to fall, we were literally knee-deep in mud. We could perceive the enemy taking up their position opposite to us, at the distance of about a mile and a-half. Their artillery began to play on us and did some, but not much, damage. One of their large shot killed two of our light company, it struck one of them in the cheek, and the other was killed with the wind of the passing ball, as effectually as if he had been struck by it.

As the storm continued, without any signs of abatement, and the night was setting in, orders were given to pile arms, but no man was on any account to quit his position. Under such circumstances our prospect of a night's lodging was anything but cheering; the only provision we had, being the remnant of the salt provision, served out on the 16th. Having disposed of that, we began to consider in what way to pass the night; to lie down was out of the question, and to stand up all night was almost equally so. We endeavoured to light some fires, but the rain soon put them out, and the only plan we could adopt was, to gather arms-full of the standing corn, and, rolling it together, made a sort of mat, on which we placed the knapsack; and sitting on that, each man holding his blanket over his head to keep off the rain, which was almost needless, as we were so thoroughly drenched:— however, this was the plan generally adopted and maintained during the night.

Some outline [*outlying*] pickets were sent out, and we could both see and hear the French, who, regardless of the weather, appeared to be very active during the night, in making their arrangements for the next day; and as sleep was altogether not to be expected, we passed the time in discussing the occurrences of the last two days, and the probable issue of the next day's contest, which we had every reason to suspect would be a most desperate one.

Our position was an extremely good defensive one, and this was not the first time it had been selected as such, for the French army occupied the very same ground, in 1705, when they were attacked and beaten by the confederate army, under the Duke of Marlborough; and again, the Prince of Orange, in 1791-5, availed himself of the same position, to cover Brussels against the advancing French Republican forces, but he was driven from it that time by the impetuosity of the enemy: so that, as far as the selection of ground went, we were very favourably circumstanced.

VII

But see, the haughty Cuirassiers advance,
The dread of Europe and the pride of France!
The war's whole art—each private soldier knows,
And with a general's love of conquest glows;
Contempt and fury fire their souls by turns,
Each nation's glory in each warrior burns,
Each fights, as in *his* arm the important day,
And all the fate of his great monarch lay.

About daybreak, on the morning of the 18th, the rain subsided, and we began to light fires with such materials as we could get from the forest, and with the straw of the corn, which was still standing in considerable quantities. By six o'clock we had a cloudless sky and a powerful sun, under the cheering influence of which, we began to clean our muskets for the coming strife. Having shaved myself and put on a clean shirt, I felt tolerably comfortable, though many around me were complaining much of cramps and agues.

I went as far as the farmhouse of La Haye-Sainte, and obtained some water, and on returning had an excellent view of the arrangements made by the antagonist forces. As the morning wore on, brigade-majors and aides-de-camps were riding about, with instructions from the Duke, to each division and brigade, to take up its proper position for the day.

The Foot Guards were on the right of the line, and a portion of them were detached to occupy and defend the château of Hugamont, a post of the utmost importance, as the possession of that by the enemy would have enabled them to turn our right flank; next the Guards, was the 33rd and 69th, which formed one square together, then the 30th and our regiment, the 73rd, formed the next square. Sufficient room was of course left between the squares, to enable the troops to deploy into line when necessary. Immediately on our left was a regiment of Dutch infantry; next to them were other regiments of British infantry. The farm-house was occupied by a strong body of Hanoverians; the left of our line was formed on the other side of the Brussels road, and the whole extended about a mile and a-half.

The regiment of Dutch infantry above was, in fact, Kielmansegge's 1st Hanoverian Brigade. At the outset this post, the farmhouse at La Haye Sainte, was large enough to hold 1,000 men but was only held by Major Baring and the 2nd Light Battalion of the King's German Legion, some 376 strong. The brigade of German artillery mentioned below was Cleeve's Field Brigade (six- and nine-pounders) KGL.

Our artillery, which was strong and effective, was very judiciously placed, and did great execution. A brigade of German artillery formed on the ridge, just in front of our brigade, and was taken on the first advance of the cuirassiers. Two divisions of the British, and most of the Nassau troops, were placed in the rear, forming another line; and it was supposed that more than ten thousand of these were killed or wounded, without having the opportunity of firing a shot. The Life Guards and Oxford Blues[1] were in the rear of the squares, and the rest of the cavalry were disposed of in the same way along the lines. The light companies of the different regiments were ordered in front, to co-operate with the Rifles, in skirmishing with the enemy.

As my brother was going on this duty, we shook hands, not supposing it likely that we should both be preserved through such a battle as this promised to be. From this time we had no opportunity of seeing each other until the close of the action.

By twelve o'clock the artillery on both sides were busily engaged. Some commissariat waggons came into the field, with a supply of salt provisions and spirits, and two men from each company were sent for them. I was one of these. It was some time before I got our allowance of hollands; and we had scarcely received it, when a cannon-shot went through the cask, and man too. While waiting here, [*Corporal John*] Shaw, the fighting-man, of the [*2nd*] Life Guards, was pointed out to me; and we little thought then, that he was about to acquire such celebrity. He drank a considerable portion of the raw spirit; and under the influence of that probably, he soon afterwards left his regiment, and running 'a-muck' at the enemy, was cut down by them as a madman.

I admire as much as any man can do, individual acts of bravery, but

---

[1] Royal Regiment of Horse Guards.

Shaw certainly falls very far short of my definition of the term *hero*.
The path of duty is the path of safety; and it is quite likely that Shaw,
if he had remained with his regiment, might have exercised his skill,
courage, and stamina, quite as effectively against the foe, without the
certainty of losing his own life; and to rush, in such a way, on to
certain death, was, in my opinion, as much an act of suicide, as if he
had plunged with his horse from the cliffs of Dover. In 'union there
is strength', but if every man were to follow Shaw's example—quit
his regiment and seek distinction for himself—there would be an end
to all discipline, and, consequently, to all chance of success.

I am glad to have it in my power to record acts of heroism, on the
part of some of the Life Guards, who were satisfied with doing their
duty, without madly throwing their own lives away.

Having returned to our regiment, and distributed the usual allowance of spirits to the company, I had three canteens full left; being the
allowance for those men who had been placed *hors-de-combat*. I took
an extra drop with my old friend Sergeant Burton; and he ordered
me to keep some to drink together after the battle. I told him, I
thought very few of us would live to see the close of that day: when
he said, 'Tom, I'll tell you what it is; there is no shot made yet for
either you or me.'

As the enemy's artillery was taking off a great many of our men,
we were ordered to lie down, to avoid the shots as much as possible;
and I took advantage of this circumstance to obtain an hour's sleep,
as comfortably as ever I did in my life, though there were at that time
upwards of three hundred cannon in full play. But our services were
now soon to be required. A considerable number of the French
cuirassiers made their appearance, on the rising ground just in our
front, took the artillery we had placed there, and came at a gallop
down upon us. Their appearance, as an enemy, was certainly enough
to inspire a feeling of dread,—none of them under six feet; defended
by steel helmets and breastplates, made pigeon-breasted to throw off
the balls. Their appearance was of such a formidable nature, that I
thought we could not have the slightest chance with them. They came
up rapidly, until within about ten or twelve paces of the square,
when our rear ranks poured into them a well-directed fire, which put
them into confusion, and they retired; the two front ranks, kneeling,
then discharged their pieces at them. Some of the cuirassiers fell
wounded, and several were killed; those of them that were dismounted
by the death of their horses, immediately unclasped their armour to

facilitate their escape. The next square to us, was charged at the same time, and were unfortunately broken into and retired in confusion, followed by the cuirassiers; but the Life Guards coming up, the French in their turn, were obliged to retrogade, and the 33rd and 69th resumed their position in square, on our right, and maintained it during the rest of the day.

The Duke of Wellington came up to us, after this, and while speaking to General Halket, the cuirassiers again advanced. The Duke rode into the square, and we again sent them to the right-about; and the Horse Guards came out at the intervals, and followed the cuirassiers some distance; but did not then come actually in contact with them. The Duke rode out of the square, and paid a visit to the Guards, on the right, after expressing himself perfectly satisfied with our conduct. My comrade, whom I have already spoken of, as being quartered with me at the village near Soignes, was on my right hand, in the front face of the square in the front rank, kneeling; he had a trifling defect in his speech; at every charge the cavalry made, he would say, 'Tom, Tom, here comes the *calvary*'.

The same body of the enemy, though baffled twice, seemed determined to force a passage through us; and on their next advance, they brought some artillery-men, turned the cannon in our front upon us, and fired into us with grape-shot, which proved very destructive, making complete lanes through us; and then the horsemen came up to dash in at the openings. But before they reached, we had closed our files, throwing the dead outside, and taking the wounded inside the square; and they were again forced to retire. They did not, however, go further than the pieces of cannon—waiting there to try the effect of some more grape-shot. We saw the match applied, and again it came thick as hail upon us. On looking round, I saw my left hand man falling backwards, the blood gushing from his left eye; my poor comrade on my right, also by the same discharge, got a ball through his right thigh, of which he died a few days afterwards.

Our situation, now, was truly awful; our men were falling by dozens every fire. About this time, also, a large shell fell just in front of us, and while the fuze was burning out, we were wondering how many of us it would destroy. When it burst, about seventeen men were either killed or wounded by it; the portion which came to my share, was a piece of rough cast-iron, about the size of a horse-bean, which took up its lodging in my left cheek; the blood ran copiously down inside my clothes, and made me rather uncomfortable. Our poor old captain was horribly frightened; and several times came to me for a drop of something to keep his spirits up. Towards the close of the day, he was cut in two by a cannon shot.

The next charge the cavalry made, they deliberately walked their horses up to the bayonet's point; and one of them, leaning over his horse, made a thrust at me with his sword. I could not avoid it, and involuntarily closed my eyes. When I opened them again, my enemy was lying just in front of me, within reach, in the act of thrusting at me. He had been wounded by one of my rear rank men, and whether it was the anguish of the wound, or the chagrin of being defeated, I know not; but he endeavoured to terminate his existence with his own sword: but that being too long for his purpose, he took one of our bayonets, which was lying on the ground, and raising himself up with one hand, he placed the point of the bayonet under his cuirass, and fell on it.

The cuirassiers now transferred their favours to some other quarter, and left us at liberty to contemplate the havock they had made; and the Duke of Wellington riding by, again addressed our general with, 'Well Halket, how do you get on?' The general replied, 'My Lord, we are dreadfully cut up; can you not relieve us for a little while?' 'Impossible,' said the Duke. 'Very well, my Lord', said the general; 'we'll stand till the last man falls!'

The next time the cuirassiers made their appearance in our front, the Life Guards boldly rode out from our rear to meet them, and in point of numbers, they seemed pretty well matched. The French waited, with the utmost coolness, to receive them, opening their ranks to allow them to ride in. As they were so close, and we had nothing to do at the time, we had a fine opportunity of seeing them, and were much pleased to find the Life Guards so good a match for them; and we wondered why they had not been led against them earlier in the day.

It was a fair fight, and the French were fairly beaten and driven off. I noticed one of the Guards, who was attacked by two cuirassiers, at the same time; he bravely maintained the unequal conflict for a minute or two, when he disposed of one of them by a deadly thrust in the throat. His combat with the other one lasted about five minutes, when the guardsman struck his opponent a slashing back-handed stroke, and sent his helmet some distance, with the head inside it. The horse galloped away with the headless rider, sitting erect in the saddle, the blood spouting out of the arteries like so many fountains.

Hitherto, we had acted only against cavalry, but now Napoleon was leading up his infantry, in masses; and as our brigade was literally cut to pieces, the remnant was formed into line four-deep. But the French infantry, that were now advancing, were so overwhelming in numbers, that we were forced to retire; while doing so, General Halket received a musket ball through his cheek, and falling from his horse, was taken to the rear.

The fire from the French infantry was so tremendous that our brigade divided, and sought shelter behind some banks; and I here again met my brother. He had been taken prisoner in the early part of the day, but released himself, and made good his retreat to the square of the Guards, where he remained during one charge of the cavalry, and then he joined his own regiment; but as his company was in a different face of the square to mine, we had not, till now, had an opportunity of seeing each other.

The only captain we now had left, invited us from the shelter of the bank, to follow him in an attack on about three thousand of the French infantry. About a dozen of us accepted the invitation; and such was the destructive fire to which we were opposed, that we had not advanced more than six or seven paces, before every one of the party, except me and my brother, was either killed or wounded. We carried the captain back to the shelter of the bank, where we found our first major [*Dawson Kelly*], who had not been with us during the day, having been attached to the staff. He ordered the captain to be taken to the rear, and then caused us to be mustered. We numbered two officers and seventy men; the battalion, when we entered the field the first day, had twenty-nine officers and five hundred and fifty men. My worthy friend, Burton, gave me a hearty slap on the back, and said, 'Out with the grog, Tom; did I not tell you there was no shot made for you or me?'

At this time, the old French Guard having been driven back, the welcome news spread like wildfire along the line, that the Prussians had arrived; and orders were given for a general charge along the whole line. While we were forming four deep for this purpose, Major Kelly ordered our colours (which had been completely riddled, and almost separated from the staff,) to be taken from the staff, and they were rolled round the body of a trusty sergeant (Weston), with instruction to take them to Brussels for safety, as we no longer had any officer to carry them. We then advanced with the line; but not far, as the Prussians took upon themselves the task of pursuing the enemy; so we returned to within about fifty yards of the spot we had been fighting on all day.

We regretted much the loss of our second Major, McLean,[1] who had joined us some months before, from the first battalion in the East Indies, where he had been sixteen years. He was a Scotchman, and was most deservedly popular with the men, for his urbanity and humanity. His servant, Duncan Campbell, also a Scotchman, had been with him during the whole of his Indian service, and obtained permission to join the 2nd Battalion with the major, and he was killed nearly at the same time with his beloved master.

Our sergeant-major was a brave soldier, and had been through the whole of the engagements in the Peninsula, with the 43rd regiment. During the day, when our men were falling so very fast, he turned deadly pale, and said to the colonel, 'We had nothing like this in Spain, Sir.' The worst fault he had, was an inveterate habit of swearing, which he could not avoid, even under these awful circumstances. Noticing one of the men, named Dent, stopping every now and then, as the shots came whizzing by, he said 'D——n you, Sir; what do you lie there for? You should not lie down if you head was off!'

When we were ordered to retire from the French infantry, a young man belonging to us, named Steel, a lad of rare courage, was in the act of firing, when a cannon shot, in rolling along the ground, took his foot off at the ankle. He did not fall, but advancing a step on his shattered stump, said, 'D——n you, I'll serve you out for that!' and fired his piece among the enemy.

While we were retiring, Sergeant Mure, of the Grenadiers, a very brave and good solider, in turning round to have a look at the enemy, received a musket ball in the forehead, and fell on his back a corpse. A cousin of his, named Morrison, on hearing of his death, ran back in the face of a most destructive fire, to where his cousin lay, kissed his cheek, let fall a tear or two, and then joined us again.

Of one of the officers of the 30th, who, when we were laying together at the village near Soignes, I recollected one of our men observing that 'he would be a decent-sized fellow, if his legs were taken off.' I thought of the remark, when I saw the officer lying with both legs broke, just below the knees, by a cannon ball. He requested me to cut off his legs, but I had not the heart to do it, though it would have been an act of mercy; for when I saw him next morning, he was in the same situation, having had no assistance.

[1] Archibald John Maclean. Died of wounds at Brussels.

While we had any daylight left, I went among my wounded comrades, rendering all the assistance in my power, binding up some of their wounds, and placing them in more easy positions. All their cry was for 'Water'; but alas! we had none to give them; we were ourselves suffering the most intolerable thirst, from the heat of the weather, the exertion and the salt provisions. The cries and shrieks of the poor creatures would have been dreadful in the night, if we could have heard them; but the continued discharges of the artillery, during the battle, had so affected the drums of the ears, that we could scarcely hear anything for two or three days afterwards, but the roaring of cannon.

We lay on the ground that night. I fell asleep, but awoke again about midnight, almost mad, for want of water, and I made up my mind to go in search of some. By the light of the moon, I picked my way among the bodies of my sleeping, as well as of my dead comrades; but, the horrors of the scene created such a terror in my mind, that I could not muster courage to go by myself, and was turning back to get my brother along with me, when on passing where a horse was lying dead, on its side, and a man sitting upright with his back against the horse's belly, I thought I heard the man call to me, and the hope that I could render him some assistance, overcame my terror. I went towards him, and placing my left hand on his shoulder, intended to lift him up with my right; my hand, however, passed through his body, and I then saw that both he and his horse had been killed by a cannon ball.

I now fairly ran back again to my resting-place, and arousing my brother, begged of him to go with me for water. The thought struck us that we might find some among our comrades, who were sleeping around. We came at last to a man named Smith, who, for his foraging propensities, was called 'Cossack Smith',—the man I have before alluded to, as refusing some potatoes to an officer in Germany. Well, on sounding his canteen, we found it full of water, and he was sleeping with his head upon it, and the strap passed round his body. The strap we unbuckled; and gently raising his head, we substituted an empty canteen for the full one, and retired to the spot where we had been previously lying.

We, between us, emptied the canteen, and flung it from us; and then laid down and slept till sunrise, when the first sound we heard was Smith, blustering and swearing about the loss of his water; and threatening, if he knew who had taken it, he would run him through;

and I knew sufficiently of the man, to believe he would do so. In order to satisfy my own conscience about the matter, I offered him a portion of the spirits, out of my canteen; he took it, but observed, that spirits then was not like water. As he was of a very revengeful disposition, we thought it prudent to keep him in the dark, as to who the thieves were.

I passed some time, in the morning, in looking for my wounded comrade, and not finding him, I was in hopes that he had been conveyed to Brussels; but I was sorry afterwards to learn, that he lay for a day and a night, without having his wound dressed, and that, when he was removed to Brussels, mortification had taken place, and he died raving mad.

Among the list of the killed, on the 18th, was poor Jack Parsons, one of the best-hearted, good-humoured, generous, fellows, that I ever met with. He was a native of Staffordshire, and invariably carried with him, in his knap-sack, the last gift of his poor old mother, consisting of a piece of bacon, which he preserved with as much care as if it had been the most valuable relic.

Poor Jack was so fond of drink, that he was always getting into some scrape, and passed a great deal of his time in the guard-room, as a prisoner. His frolics, however, when inebriated, were of so perfectly good-humoured and harmless a nature, that he never received any more severe punishment than confinement to the guard-room, with extra guards, drills, and stoppage of grog—the last, to him the worst punishment of all.

When any of the men were to be deprived of their grog, it was generally spilt in the front of the company; and on one occasion, as the officer was in the act of turning out Jack's allowance from a canteen, the poor fellow cast an anxious glance at the precious liquid, as it trickled on the ground, and adopted the following expedient, to save, at least a portion of it. Turning his eyes in a direction behind the officer, he said, 'Here's the general coming, Sir'; the officer turned sharply round, to see where, and in the meantime Jack had both hands under the canteen, receiving as much as they would contain, and conveying it to his mouth. The officer could not help laughing at the ingenuity of the trick, and generously returned him the canteen, with a portion of the spirit remaining in it.

On another occasion, when marching through Germany, we were for some days without our usual supply of spirits, from the utter inability of the quartermaster to obtain it. Some German Hussars were marching in the same direction with us, and as is usual with them on the line of march, were singing in chorus. Our colonel not being acquainted with the German language, said to an officer, with whom he was riding, 'I wonder what they are singing about?' Jack immediately replied, in the hearing of the colonel, 'I know what they are singing about!' 'Well, Jack,' said the colonel, 'let's hear what it is.' 'Why', said Jack 'they are singing—

> We have got schn-a-a-ps,
> And the 73rd have got no-o-one.'

The hint was not thrown away, for the colonel said, laughing, 'Well Jack, we'll try and get you some schnaps tonight.'

When we were at Antwerp, Jack formed an acquaintance with a very pretty Flemish girl, to whom he became much attached, and she conducted herself with so much propriety, that the officers suffered her to accompany the regiment, as her companionship with Jack had such a beneficial effect on his conduct.

On the morning of the 18th, at Waterloo, Jack presented himself before his captain, and requested his signature to his last will and testament—simply a request that the arrears of pay due to him, might be given to his 'Poor Therese'. There was such a marked difference in Jack's countenance, that the officer was induced to enquire the reason, and he stated 'that during the night, as he lay on the ground, his poor old mother (recently dead) had appeared, and solemnly assured him, that the day would be his last. The captain could not help smiling at his superstitious fears, but, at the same time, assured him that his request should be attended to, if he fell: Jack then expressed himself satisfied, but the seriousness of his countenance, so unusual to him, exposed him to the raillery of his comrades. Jack was no coward, and the impression which the dream had left on his mind, did not prevent him doing his duty. When the roll was called at night, Jack was reported 'killed'.

A few days afterwards, poor Therese joined us, on our way to Paris, and went nearly distracted at the loss of her 'Dear Jack'. She continued to journey with us, and the men treated her very kindly. When we reached Paris, and were at camp, at the Bois de Boulogne, some benevolent Parisian ladies interested themselves in her behalf, and obtained for her a comfortable situation, as servant to a respectable family in Passe [Passy]; who, being made acquainted with her history, treated her with the utmost kindness.

A great deal has been said and written, as to the probable result of the battle of the 18th, if the Prussians had not arrived; and, if the opinion of so humble an individual as myself can have any weight, I would say, most decidedly, we could have maintained our ground; nor would it have been possible for the enemy, unless strongly reinforced, to have driven us from our strong defensive position.

The expected arrival of Marshal Grouchy, to join Napoleon, or of the Prussians, to aid the English, could have made very little difference in the calculation, as they were in view of each other; and if Grouchy had joined the French, Blücher would not have been far off, so that it could only have given an accession of numbers to each party, without altering their relative position. The non-arrival of Grouchy in the field, is accounted for, by the fact of his being out-generaled by his vigilant antagonist Blücher; who, leaving a portion of his troops to amuse the French general, pushed on the main body of his army to assist the British, at Waterloo, according to a previous arrangement, between him and Wellington.

But while I thus contend we could not have been beaten, I feel bound, at the same time, to admit that the battle was decided by the Prussians; and but for their prompt arrival, and vigorous pursuit of the enemy, Napoleon would probably have fallen back to join Grouchy, and to have received some reinforcements from France, when he would have been able to resume offensive operations against us. But, even then, he would have had no chance of ultimate success, considering the vast amount of troops that were pouring into France from every direction.

In the brief description I have given of the battle, my observations have been limited to the brigade in which I was engaged; but if any of my readers should feel desirous of more copious information, I would beg to refer them to the accounts furnished by a French officer, which may be found in 'Kelly's' history of the battle;[1] which is, in my opinion, the very best narrative of the transactions extant. The only error I can discover in it, is where he attributes the defeat of Marshal Ney, on the 16th, at Quatre Bras, to the vigorous attack of the British cavalry, whereas, it is notorious that the English had no cavalry at all in the field that day.

In the forenoon of the 19th, our brigade was ordered to fall in, and the four regiments did not muster more than six hundred men.

[1] Christopher Kelly, *History of the French Revolution and of the Wars Produced by That Memorable Event* (London, 1817).

The general being wounded, the command of the brigade devolved on Colonel Elphinstone,[1] of the 33rd; and under his command we immediately commenced our march over the field of battle, in the track of the enemy.

In the field itself, it was supposed there were about forty thousand dead bodies of men, and ten thousand horses; but on our march, this day, for the distance of about twelve miles, the roads were thickly strewn with the dead and dying. But before I go any further, I shall subjoin a list of the number of officers killed and wounded, in the three days; and, as the loss of officers is generally a criterion of the loss of men, it will be seen, that though no mention has been made of us, either in the Duke's despatches, or in the histories of the battle extant, yet it will from that list be seen, that we actually suffered more than any other corps in the field—pretty good evidence that we were sharply engaged.

In the following list, to which I beg to call the reader's attention, it will be found there are only three regiments who lost more officers than the 73rd, and those three, it must be remembered, were first battalions and, consequently, stronger than us by one-third. If this circumstance is borne in mind, it will then be evident that our loss was actually greater than any other corps in the battle, either British or foreign. The 33rd and 42nd are also first battalions, and their loss was the same as ours. The Foot Guards, who have had the most praise for their bravery, it appears, lost sixty-three officers, but then there were five battalions of them, each stronger considerably than our regiments; so that their loss averages little more than twelve officers to each battalion, and yet, they were reported to have been cut to pieces. But the household troops are most expensive to the nation, and their superior efficiency must therefore be upheld, though at the expense of truth.

LIST OF OFFICERS KILLED AND WOUNDED IN THE THREE DAYS

	Battalion	Killed	Wounded	Total
1st Regt of Foot Guards	2	5	10	15
1st Guards	3	4	12	16
Royal Scots (*sic*)	3	0	12	12
Coldstream Guards	2	1	7	8

[1] Lt-Colonel William Keith Elphinstone, to those incompetence the disastrous retreat from Kabul in 1841 may be attributed.

	Battalion	Killed	Wounded	Total
3rd Regt of Guards	2	3	9	12
1st Foot	3	8	13	21
4th Foot	1	0	9	9
14th Foot	3	0	1	1
23rd Foot	1	4	6	10
27th Foot	1	2	13	15
28th Foot		1	17	18
30th Foot	2	6	13	19
32nd Foot	1	1	30	31
33rd Foot	1	5	17	22
40th Foot	1	2	11	13
42nd Foot		3	19	22
44th Foot	2	2	18	20
51st Foot		0	2	2
52nd Foot		1	8	9
69th Foot	2	4	7	11
71st Foot		1	14	15
73rd Foot	2	6	16	22[1]

[1] These figures of Morris agree with C. Kelly's in *Battle of Waterloo*.

16 AUGUST 1815	17 AUGUST	18 AUGUST
wounded	*killed*	*killed*
Lieut. J. Lloyd	J. Acres (d. of w.)	Captains A. Robertson
Ensigns T. Deacon (severely)	*wounded*	J. Kennedy
R. Hesselridge	W. Strachan	Lieut. M. Hollis
(slightly)		Ensigns S. Lowe
		C. Page
		wounded
		Lieut.-Col W. G. Harris
		(severely)
		Major A. M'Lean (severely)
		Captains H. Coane
		W. Wharton
		J. Garland (severely)
		Lieuts J. McConnel
		T. Reynolds (severely)
		D. Browne (severely)
		Ensigns W. M'Bean (severely)
		C. Eastwoode
		(slightly)
		C. Bridge (severely)
		P. Hay (severely)

Totals: killed—6; wounded—16

	Battalion	Killed	Wounded	Total
79th Foot	1	3	28	31
92nd Foot	1	5	26	31
95th Foot	1	1	16	17
95th Foot	2	0	14	14
95th Foot	3	0	4	4
1st Life Guards		2	4	6
2nd Life Guards		1	0	1
1st Dragoon Guards		3	4	7
1st Royal Dragoons		4	9	13
2nd or R.N.B. Dragoons		6	8	14
1st Light Dragoons		3	11	14
2nd Light Dragoons		2	5	7
11th Light Dragoons		1	5	6
12th Light Dragoons		2	3	5
13th Light Dragoons		1	9	10
16th Light Dragoons		2	4	6
23rd Light Dragoons		0	5	5
6th Dragoons		1	5	6
1st Hussars		0	1	1
3rd Hussars		4	8	12
7th Hussars		0	7	7
10th Hussars		2	6	8
15th Hussars		2	7	9
18th Hussars		0	2	2
Royal Regiment Horse Guards (Blue)		1	4	5
Royal Artillery		4	8	12
Royal Artillery F.G.L.		1	5	6
Royal Artillery, British		0	12	12
Royal Engineers		0	1	1
Royal Staff Corps		0	2	0

VIII

So now the business of the field is o'er,
The trumpets sleep, and cannons cease to roar,
When every dismal echo is decay'd,
And all the thunder of the battle laid

On the 19th, we proceeded about sixteen miles towards France, and entered a town, the name of which I have forgotten. We were billeted on the inhabitants, and obtained from our commissariat a supply of fresh provisions. I here got my wounded cheek dressed, and the piece of iron extracted; I kept it for some time, and intended to have preserved it, as a momento of the battle, but I lost it afterwards at Paris. After a good night's rest, which to us was quite a luxury, we proceeded next day on our march. On entering France, an order was issued, by the Duke, strictly prohibiting the British from taking anything from the inhabitants, without paying for it.

Our progress through France, was of the most rapid nature, as it was important to reach Paris, before the scattered French troops could rally. Our brigade obtained no more quarters on the road, but were taken, on an average, about thirty miles a day, which was tolerably good travelling, considering the heat of the weather and the weight we had to carry,—viz. musket, accoutrements, knapsack, canteen, camp-kettle, blankets, greatcoat, haversack, and provisions, and about 120 rounds of ball cartridge; making altogether about 60 lbs, which the infantry have each to carry.

On this march they generally took us as far as we were able to go, and then turned us into a field, or wood, to bivouack for the night, there to remain, like so many sheep, until we were called in the morning to resume the march. It was considered, that a great deal of unnecessary severity was practised towards the men; provost guards were appointed to follow in the rear, and they had orders to flog every man they found behind his regiment, without a written pass from his officer.

These harassing marches continued from the 19th to the 27th, when we reached the environs of Paris, and opened a communication with Blücher, who had arrived there first, with the Prussian army. It was thought we should still have our work to do, as the strong posts, at Mont Martre, were occupied with a large body of French troops. A summons, however, was sent to the authorities of Paris, requiring them to give up the keys, in three days, or the place would be stormed by the English and Prussian forces.

The second day was Sunday, and such was the thoughtless, volatile disposition of the Parisians, that every theatre in Paris was literally crammed that evening, by the votaries of pleasure, with the horrors of war suspended over them. The utter hopelessness of any further opposition, induced the ruling powers to surrender, and we entered Paris on the 3rd of July, the British troops marching through, and forming a camp in the Bois de Boulogne. No English troops were quartered in Paris; that privilege was reserved for the Prussians. The first week, we had full employment in cutting down trees, fixing tents, and forming parade grounds. We had the pleasure here again to receive our colours, and we were joined by a good many, whose wounds were only of a slight nature.

I have stated, that on the 18th, a man on my left hand, was struck by a ball in the left eye, and fell backwards; and having thus seen him fall, I, when the roll was called, stated that he was killed; judge then my surprise, when he joined us at Paris! The ball was still in his head, and could not be extracted; he was not fit for duty, and was sent to England, where he died a few months afterwards. We received here a reinforcement of officers. Our colonel, the present Lord Harris, was badly wounded, and never joined us again. Being joined by a detachment of men from our depôt, we began again to assume an appearance of strength.

The 69th regiment, in order to remove from themselves the disgrace of having lost their king's colour, at Quatre Bras, set their tailors secretly to work and manufactured a new colour, and then contradicted the statement of their having lost one. But, unfortunately for them, Napoleon, in his dispatches to Paris, had noticed the capture of this colour, and the colour itself was forwarded to Paris and exhibited there. It was a great pity the 69th adopted such a plan, for though it is unfortunate in a regiment to lose its colours, yet, if taken while they are contending with a vastly superior force, as was the case in this instance, it cannot reflect any disgrace on the men.

We had now a supply of regular canvas tents, quite new, and being regularly arranged in lines, they presented a very pretty appearance, and we were visited by thousands of the Parisians, who did not seem to consider it any disgrace, to have a foreign army, at camp, so close to them. The English soldiers were not allowed in Paris at all, except by a written pass, signed by the commanding officer, and this was not to be given but under special circumstances.

My brother was on the provost-guard, in the village of Passe, and he had an order to enter Paris. As I had a very strong desire to go also, I contrived to include my name in the pass, with his; and though we were interrogated by the officer of the guard (Prussians) on entering, the addition was not noticed, and we got in and spent a very comfortable day, examining the palaces and other public buildings, and drinking during the day about a dozen bottles of wine, for which we paid as many francs! When night came, and we ought to have been returning to camp, we took it in our heads to go to the theatre, where some of the partisans of Napoleon strove to pick a quarrel with us, and we should have been roughly handled, but for the arrival of some gen-d'armes, who gave us some very good advice, namely, to make the best of our way home; advice which we thought it would be prudent to follow, as it was getting late, and we were absent without leave. We thought to avoid the patrols, by riding in a hackney coach, as far as the outer gate, but the coachman refused to take us. We insisted he should, and got in; the coachman shut the door, and taking out his horses, left us there by ourselves. We were now compelled to make the best of our way on foot; and in going over one of the bridges, we met a Prussian patrol, who took us prisoners.

On reaching their guard-room, we were first examined by the officer of the guard, and afterwards by the Commandant of Paris, a Prussian prince. We thought it better to be without a pass, than to exhibit the one we had, so stated we had entered with a pass, but had unfortunately lost it. The prince said, he was sorry to be under the necessity of detaining us till morning. I then requested he would send us to the main-guard, which I recollected had been furnished that day by our own regiment. This he readily complied with; and sent us directly, under an escort, and we were handed over to the sergeant of the main-guard; and lying down on the guard-bed, we soon fell asleep.

At six o'clock in the morning, the guard roused us up with his sword, and told us to make the best of our way home, as there was no crime set against us. The Prussians, probably, were not aware of the fact, that an officer, or non-commissioned officer, on guard in the English service, is not bound to detain any man as prisoner more than an hour, unless a written charge is lodged against him; and our officer, who was friendly towards us, took advantage of the circumstance, and set us free.

My brother, if he could get to Passe, was in no danger; and as soon as I reached the camp, I went to Sergeant Burton, who, I was glad to hear, had not reported my absence: as he said, he knew I should not get into any scrape. On attending parade that morning, my name, among others, was among the list of promotions; and the next time I went into Paris, on guard, was as a non-commissioned officer.

The Bois de Boulogne, in which we were encamped was, when we first entered, a continuous wood, thickly planted, and extending for miles; but by the time we had been there a month, so many of the trees had been cut down, for the construction of huts, and for fire-wood, that we had ample space for parade grounds, etc.

The single men were in the tents, but the married people had huts, in a line parallel with the tents; and when the boughs of which they were formed, were fresh, they had a very rural, gipsy-like appearance.

One night, one of these huts—occupied by a sutler, being a sort of chandler's shop—caught fire, and the flames communicated so rapidly from one to the other, that within an hour, every hut of that description on that line, was consumed. The flames, carried by a brisk wind, even penetrated to the tents, which created a great deal of alarm. In each tent were eighteen men, their arms and accoutrements being fastened round the centre pole; and in each tent, in the cartridge-boxes so hanging, there were not less than two thousand ball cartridges; so that when we were awakened by the approach of the flames, we were obliged to uproot the tent by main force, carrying it out of the reach of the fire; and as we did this almost in a state of nudity, it became a matter of some difficulty with us, afterwards, to collect the several portions of our dress and clothing.

Such a circumstance, occurring in the night, created considerable alarm, not only through the camp, but also in Paris, the fire being strongly reflected in the sky. To prevent the recurrence of such fires, no huts were for the future to be erected, within a certain distance of the camp; and they were then to be built separately.

About this time, the Duke issued a general order for the whole of the British troops to pass him in review. The day selected was remarkably fine, and presented one of the most imposing spectacles ever witnessed.

The Duke, on his favourite charger, decorated, or rather loaded, with the gold and diamond insignia of the whole of the various orders, which had been conferred on him, surrounded by the Allied Sovereigns, Princes, Dukes, Generals and Aide-de-camps, took his position in an open space of ground, near the palace, and the troops marched by in open columns or companies. After passing, we went some distance through the streets of Paris, and then going out of another gate, and passing round the suburbs, came back to the spot we had started from; and though we had gone, probably, a distance of five miles, we came upon the rear of those who had not yet passed.

The streets in Paris were densely crowded, and the windows and tops of houses filled with well, but gaudily-dressed females, waving their handkerchiefs, and greeting our troops as they passed with the strongest manifestations of joy. Our regiment was fortunate in passing so soon, as we got back, and were dismissed long before the review terminated.

In the order-book, next day, the Duke expressed his perfect satisfaction with the appearance of the army.

The next time I mounted guard in Paris, at the Duke de Berri's establishment; and I had an opportunity of witnessing the removal of the celebrated Group of Horses, of which Napoleon had despoiled the Venetians, and which were now about to be restored. The Horses, which had been placed over the entrance to the palace, were, with much difficulty and labour, lowered into small waggons or cars, under a strong guard of English and Prussians.

The Parisians, who had assembled in considerable numbers, looked on in gloomy silence; and when the last Horse was safely deposited, one of Napoleon's old veterans exclaimed, 'Now, I have nothing left to give my children, but my eternal hatred of the English!' 'And that,' said an English gentleman who was standing by, and understood the language; 'that will do your children no good, and England no harm.'

But their humiliation was not yet complete. The celebrated gallery of pictures, selected by Buonaparte, at the various places he had conquered, and deposited in the palace of St Cloud, were claimed by the respective parties from whom they had been plundered, and the restoration of them determined on. I was on duty at the palace of St

Cloud when the removal was going on, and had an opportunity of seeing some of them, but am not connoisseur enough to describe them.

The satisfaction of Louis [*XVIII*], on his restoration, must have been greatly damped by these occurrences, as well as by the fact, that he was only secure on the throne of his ancestors, so long as he was supported by foreign bayonets.

In the beginning of September, our camp at the Bois de Boulogne was broken up, and a fresh one formed between the village of St Cloud and Boulogne, better supplied with water. For several days I was on that disagreeable duty—a provost-guard, in the village of Boulogne. One night, on perambulating the streets, we met two Hanoverian soldiers, who, on being taken to the guard-room, stated they were servants, and had been on an errand for their masters. This explanation, however, did not serve them; and one of them was tied to a tree in the yard, and received three or four dozen lashes; as the other one was about being tied up, his master—who had by some means heard of his capture—arrived, and claiming him as his servant, ordered him to be released. 'And, pray,' said the provost-marshal, 'who are you, Sir?' 'I am an officer in the Hanoverian service, bearing His Majesty's commission.' 'Have you that commission with you?' said the marshal. 'No; I have not.' 'Then go about your business, or I shall flog you!' The officer, seeming glad to get away, left his servant, who was immediately tied up, and received his allowance.

Of course, these proceedings were in obedience to orders; but, they are most disgraceful to the service. The non-commissioned officers, who accept the situation of provost-marshal, seldom go back to their own regiments, but, generally get promoted in some other corps, where they take especial care, not to mention the particular duty they have been on, or they would be received, in the same way that 'Jack Ketch' would probably be, if he were to force himself into any respectable civil society.

The troops were ordered one day, for a general parade, to witness the execution of a soldier. I was on guard that morning, and therefore, not present; but, from a comrade, I learned the following particulars. Three sides of a large square having been formed, by the troops, the prisoner was brought forward by the provost-guard. A coffin was placed near him, and the proceedings of the court-martial having been read over, sentence of death was pronounced, and the man was ordered to prepare for instant execution. The guard, with their loaded muskets, were waiting only for the fatal word, when the officer commanding, intimated to the prisoner, that the Duke had been graciously pleased to pardon him. This sudden and unexpected announcement, had the effect of depriving the poor wretch of his reason, and he left the ground a *maniac*. For the benefit of such of my readers, as may wish to be informed what crime he had committed, to subject himself to such a sentence, I will relate the following story.

In the beginning of June, a number of officers and men arrived at Ostend, from various depots, to join their respective regiments. A ship's boat was conveying two officers and twenty men ashore, (they were all in marching order). All were sitting down but one man, and he could not find room. The officer, irritated at the man not sitting down when he ordered him, struck him violently with his sword, cutting through his belts, and inflicting a very serious wound on his shoulder; some of the large veins were divided, and the man lost the use of his arm.

The soldier, following the advice which was given him, lodged a complaint against the officer, and a general court-martial was held, before whom, he was charged with striking the soldier without provocation. The charge was proved by, at least, a dozen men who were in the boat; but, when the officer was called on for his defence, he produced the other officer who was with him, who swore, that the man was inciting his comrades to mutiny, that he was very insolent, and that he actually struck the officer first. Full credence being given to this statement, as it was not supposed possible that an officer and a gentleman, would deliberately perjure himself, the officer, therefore, was honourably acquitted. The soldier was then brought before another court-martial, and the same evidence being adduced against him, he was found guilty, and sentenced to be shot, subject to the approval of the Duke. The poor fellow was marched, a prisoner, through the country, and when the troops settled at Paris, he was led out to execution, with his wounded arm hanging powerless by his side. His pardon being suddenly announced to him, he was deprived of his reason. The transition was too sudden; it would have been an act of mercy, to have carried the sentence into effect. The officer who gave evidence against him, was killed at Waterloo.

Before the final breaking-up of our camp, the sight-loving people of Paris were gratified by the exhibition of a sham fight, upon a large scale, on the ground between Paris and St Denis. In going through the evolutions, no regard was paid to the nature of the ground; if we came to a wall, we must surmount it; and if we came to a stream of water, we were expected to go through it; so that by the time the affair was over, the men were so fatigued, that many of them were not able to accompany us home to camp.

In the month of October, the weather set in very cold, with sharp frost, so that it was not deemed advisable to keep us longer at camp, lying on the cold ground.

Louis now felt himself tolerably safe, from any further efforts of Napoleon, who was, by this time, approaching St Helena.

IX

Now the scene of trouble's o'er;
And, resting on our native shore,
Gay content will sweeter be,
Compared with past adversity.

On the final breaking up of the camp, some of the regiments took their departure for England; others were quartered on the small towns near Paris, and those who were to remain, as the Army of Occupation, were sent to the garrisons, in which it was intended they should continue. To prevent any further out-break against 'Louis le Désiré', as the French King was most inappropriately styled, our regiment was sent to a village called St Remy, about twenty-five miles from Paris. I had charge of twenty of our men; and we were quartered at a flour mill, where we were placed in a detached building, containing a large square room, and kitchen.

On our first meeting with the proprietor, we found that his feeling towards us was anything but friendly; nor did he disguise his sentiments towards us and our country, thinking we did not understand his language. On his denying us wood for firing, a great deal of which he had stacked for his own use, we made free with the branches of his fruit trees, which burned tolerably well; and when the gentleman found that all his swearing, bouncing, and threatening, was of no use, he kindly informed us that he would provide us with wood from his stack.

Our duty here was very light, as we had only to furnish a small regimental guard, and a beacon guard; the latter on the top of a very steep hill, thickly studded with trees and bushes, on the sides, but the top presenting a large flat surface, and here the beacon was erected. It consisted of a quantity of dry straw, on which was placed successive layers of dry faggots of wood, to the height of about twelve or fourteen feet. It was neatly thatched, and presented the appearance of a large beehive, and the guard having charge of this, placed close to it, a sentinel, with strict orders to keep his eye constantly fixed on a hill in the distance, on which another beacon was placed; and if he saw that one on fire, he was immediately to call out the guard, and the non-commissioned officer was then to fire the one he had charge of, which would have been perceived and answered by some on the other side of us. Any insurrection, or outbreak of the French, would have been thus immediately communicated to the proper authorities.

During the latter part of November, and beginning of December, when large quantities of snow descended, and the frost set in intensely severe, this guard was certainly the very coldest position I had ever been placed in; and the journey to and from this place, while the sides of the mountain were covered with snow, was both difficult and dangerous.

About the middle of December, we received the route for England. A day or two before we left the mill, one of our men had his musket stolen, and we had pretty good circumstantial evidence that the miller himself was the thief. Our commanding officer ordered the place to be searched, but without success; and the man was provided with another firelock, and put under stoppages to pay for it. By way of revenge, the man gained access to the mill, and threw a candle in, which passing between the stones, would subject the owner to very considerable expense, in putting it to rights.

The night before we left, I found the men very busy in certain operations, which, as a non-commissioned officer, I should have put a stop to, if our Landlord had been at all friendly. On our descent from the mountain guard, that day, we caught a hare: that was immediately skinned, but not being sufficient for the whole, some of the party paid a visit to where the live rabbits were kept, and obtained about half a dozen of them. The miller was also a farmer, and had a quantity of turkeys about the place; two of them were pressed into the service, and about half a dozen fowl; the whole having been stripped and cleaned, were deposited in a large copper pan, and kept boiling on the fire, till nearly done, when some vegetables and flour were added. When done, the soup, which was extremely rich and good, was distributed and disposed of, the meat was divided fairly, and placed in the haversacks, for the next day's march. To prevent discovery, the feathers were stuffed inside the hare and rabbit skins, and two of the men undertook to bury them; but not being able to open the ground, for the frost, they thought it would answer the same purpose, if they threw them in the river close by: but they forgot, that the said river was covered with ice!

The next morning we left early, and having proceeded about half way towards Versailles, we halted for refreshment. The mill party brought out their stock of poultry and game, and reserving a sufficient quantity for themselves, they distributed the rest among their comrades; and it was nearly all put out of sight, when the miller arrived, and, in a towering passion, lodged his complaint before the commanding officer. He had magnified his loss to a great extent, and if we had really taken all that he stated we had, it would have required a horse to carry it. He pointed out the men who had been quartered on him, and they were searched; but only some small portions of meat found, which they declared was part of the hare, caught on the mountain side; so the poor fellow was obliged to return, without any redress.

On reaching Versailles, we were billeted on the inhabitants. I was quartered, with one man, at a tailor's shop, and after depositing our arms and accoutrements, we went for our allowance of bread and meat. On our return, they enquired how long that was to serve us? and on our answering two days, they expressed astonishment, and the woman said, 'that quantity of meat, three pounds, would serve their whole family a week'. The supply we got was very good, and as the woman was about preparing dinner, it being early in the day, we made her a present of it, on condition we should share with them.

Having dressed myself, and put on my side-arms, I took a walk to the Palace, having heard so much about it. I could not gain admittance to the building, but strolled through the grounds, which were certainly very prettily laid out, and in the summer, when the numberless fountains are in operation, must have an enchanting effect.

On returning to my quarters, I found an excellent dinner provided; we all sat down together, and during the evening we were on the best of terms with them. They gave us a good bed, and breakfast next morning, with a portion of our own meat, to eat on the road. They had got from it, as much soup as would last them the week.

Our next day's journey, was to St Denis, where we mixed with great quantities of Napoleon's disbanded troops. They had not been divested of their arms, and our commanding officer was afraid something unpleasant would occur, as they were much exasperated against us, and seemed desirous of a cause for quarrel. The day following, we met about two thousand of them, unarmed, returning to their respective homes, many of them glad, no doubt, to have the opportunity of doing so. Some of the veterans, as they passed, threw on us a look of bold defiance.

The road, till we reached Abbeville, was tolerably good, and the weather fine; but, on leaving that celebrated town, there was a change for the worse, and we encountered a bitter north-west wind, bringing upon us abundance of snow, hail, sleet and rain, and the road became all at once very bad.

I was this day on the baggage-guard, and we had so much difficulty in getting the waggons on, that it was late at night before we reached the village, where the regiment had halted. Having given up my charge, I received a billet, by myself, on a farm-house, about a mile distant, along a wretched by-road, that was pointed out to me; and I groped my way, as well as I could, in the dark, for about half an hour, when I came to what I supposed was to be my quarters, and knocking at the gate, I was answered by a dog, which was loose in the yard, and by the sound of his voice, I thought would be rather a formidable antagonist. As no one came, I gave another intimation on the gate, of my desire to be admitted, and a lad, who had been reluctantly forced out, came to see who the intruder was. As soon as he perceived what I was, he ran back frightened, and then, three men came, dressed in blue smock-frocks and armed with thick sticks. I presented to them my billet, and was admitted. Their fears somewhat subsided, when they found I was alone; but this very circumstance made my situation anything but pleasant. On entering the room where they had been sitting, there was a cheerful turf fire burning, and some pears roasting before it. A jug of cider was on the table, of which they invited me to partake; their looks, however, being anything but pleasant. I determined to make myself as comfortable as possible, took off my great coat and accoutrements, and exhibited to them the red coat, a colour their country's troops had so often shrunk from. I made a tolerably good supper, of bread, butter, roasted pears and cider, and went to the bed pointed out to me, in the room adjoining; where, after fastening the window, and drawing the bedstead against the door, to prevent intrusion, I lay down in my clothes, with my good musket by my side, loaded, and fell asleep.

On entering the sitting room early next morning, I found only a young woman, preparing breakfast. She was rather alarmed at first, but we soon got on good terms, and when the old man and his two sons came in, we breakfasted together; and the doubts and fears of the night were all dispelled. They pestered me with a variety of questions, which my limited knowledge of the French language, made it difficult for me to answer. I could understand, however, that they paid some very flattering compliments, on the bravery of the British troops, who, they said, fought like lions. I have never yet met a Frenchman, who did not admit the valour of English troops, though it is very common for Englishmen to speak disparagingly of the French; and this is, to say the least of it, very foolish, for if they were really cowards, there would be the less merit due to us for beating them. The parting with my host and his family, was of the most amicable nature; the sons even accompanied me, into the village, and waited until our departure, when they shook me cordially by the hand, as they bade me adieu.

There was no improvement, either in the state of the weather, or in the roads, and our day's march was anything but agreeable. To make it worse, when we reached the village destined for our lodging that night, we found the persons who had been sent on to prepare the billets, had not been able to get them, in consequence of the absence of the burgomaster; and in the whole place, containing upwards of five hundred inhabitants, there was not another individual who could either read or write. It was late that night before we got disposed of.

The next day there was a great improvement in the weather, and the roads also got better. We were full of spirits, as every day's march brought us nearer to our dear country, and we felt as much joy, at the prospect of seeing old England again, as if we had been absent twenty years; there is indeed a

> Charm that's ne'er forgot,
> Which binds man to his native spot.

One of our sergeants, named Austin, a very respectable, good soldier, having been strongly recommended by the colonel, was surprised, on this day's march, by the reception of a commission, appointing him ensign and adjutant to the regiment, the adjutant (Hay), who had been badly wounded twice at Waterloo, not being able to join us.

Our new adjutant received the congratulations of both officers and men, by all of whom he was highly esteemed. Until we arrived in England, he performed the duties of adjutant in his sergeant's great-coat, with an officer's sword and sash, which he had by him. He continued to perform the duties of that situation until the reduction of the 2nd battalion, when he went on half-pay, and was never again called on service.

He resided many years in Kensington, and brought up a large family, in a very creditable manner. He died in 1843, much regretted by his family and friends. A tombstone has been erected to his memory, in Kensington churchyard, bearing the following simple but honest inscription:—

SACRED
To The Memory Of
Mr GEORGE AUSTIN
Late of High Street, Kensington.

He Entered The Army, and Obtained, By Merit,
A Commission As
ENSIGN and ADJUTANT,
In The
2nd Battalion of the 73rd Regiment.

Many who Knew Him
Can Bear Testimony To His Good Conduct As a Soldier;
His Urbanity as an Officer;
His Kindness As a Husband;
His Tenderness and Solicitude as a Parent:
His sincerity as a Friend;
And His Integrity as a Man.

He Departed This Life on the 13th April, 1843.
Aged 59.

Mrs Austin still resides in Kensington, with a portion of her large family. She was the inseparable companion of her husband, in all his travels, and her conduct was such as to obtain for her the goodwill of both officers and men; and whether as the wife of the sergeant or officer, she was the same kind, intelligent, respectable woman.

On our last day's journey towards Boulogne, where it was expected we should embark, I was despatched first, to get the billets ready; and as I was entering the town of Boulogne, I met an aide-de-camp, who instructed me to go on to Calais and get billets, as the shipping provided for us was there. On my reporting myself to the officer in command, at Calais, he said there would be no occasion for billets, as the vessels were waiting for us, and we could immediately go on board.

On the arrival of the regiment, they were allowed a couple of hours to refresh themselves, and then they were taken on board two small vessels, where there was just sitting room, (no beds), as it was expected we should not be long crossing over to Dover.

It was midnight before we had got the baggage on board, and by daylight, in the morning, we left the harbour with a fair breeze, to waft us over; but we had not proceeded far, before the wind changed dead against us, and, instead of getting over in three or four hours, as we expected, we were knocking about all day, first on one tack, and then on another, and the wind very fresh. At last, finding it altogether impossible to reach Dover, and there being strong appearances of an approaching storm, it was deemed advisable to make for the Downs, and we were so fortunate as to reach Ramsgate in safety. The storm raged with fearful violence all night, and next morning, several vessels were lying complete wrecks, just outside the harbour.

Having got all our people and baggage on shore, we proceeded, on Christmas day, to Canterbury, and from thence through Gravesend, crossing the Thames to Tilbury Fort, then through Billericay, Chelmsford, and on to Colchester. It was Sunday when we were going into the latter place: our depôt had been there ever since we left.

Before we entered the town, it was suggested that we ought to be decorated with laurel, and, on passing a gentleman's grounds, where there was plenty of it growing, he was civilly requested to allow us to take some, telling him the purpose for which it was wanted. He not only gave a peremptory refusal, but also applied to us the term 'Vagabonds'. On the circumstance being reported to our commanding officer, he told us he would halt for half an hour, to allow us to get laurel, and an intimation was pretty plainly given that we might get it at the ground we had just passed. The hint was taken; and most of the men supplied themselves, not only with a sufficient quantity for their colours and caps, but brought away nearly all there was, and scattered it along the road.

The inhabitants of Colchester expected us, and came out, in large numbers, to welcome us back; and we passed through the town with the band playing, and the shattered colours, with the word 'Waterloo', in large gold letters, flying. We went to the barracks, and had—what we much wanted—a few days' repose. We had been away just two years and six months, and had seen as much active service in that time, as many regiments do in a ten or twenty years' absence. I had it in my power to boast, that during the time we had been away, I had not been absent from the regiment a single day.

Myself and brother obtained leave to visit London, leaving directions where a letter would find us, if we should be wanted. We found our relatives and friends all well, and received a hearty welcome from our acquaintances. We had only been at home a week, when we received orders to return immediately to Colchester, as the regiment had orders to proceed to Nottingham, there being, at that time, some disturbances in the manufacturing districts.

Once more, then, we left home, and reached Colchester the night before the regiment marched. Our road lay through Cambridgeshire and Lincolnshire; and the frost breaking up at the time, made it almost as unpleasant as our journey through France, only, that we obtained better accommodation, and the people everywhere behaved towards us with the utmost kindness, the word 'Waterloo' having a magic influence in our favour. The roads in Lincolnshire were almost impassable, for the floods; and we were very glad when we reached Nottingham, which was intended to be the headquarters of our regiment; six companies remaining there, two going on to Dudley, and two to Wolverhampton. My company was ordered to the latter place, and I was sent a day before, to obtain the billets.

The people at Wolverhampton were all excitement, when they heard that part of a Waterloo regiment was coming among them; and as soon as I had announced myself to the constable, whose duty it was to prepare the billets, he gave me one on the 'Eagle and Child', a decent public-house, near the old church-yard, and when the news circulated, that one of the Waterloo men was actually there, people flocked in in such numbers, that the house could not accommodate them. Hundreds of them shook hands with me, and if I could have eaten and drank gold, I might have had it. The house was kept open very late that night, and I was obliged to remain, explaining the nature and circumstances of the battle; and was not sorry when the house closed, and I was suffered to go to bed. The next morning, the house of the constable was beset by publicans, who, instead of striving, as they do in London, to shift the burden from them, were anxious to have men billeted on them, finding that it would, for a time, bring 'grist to the mill'.

Our two companies, on their arrival, were welcomed into the town, and on receiving their billets, were followed to their respective quarters, and treated liberally; and many of them were too bashful to say when they had enough, so that it was several days before we could get anything like order among them. The captain commanding, was,

however, very good, and dispensed with parading until the excitement should subside. He also, and the other officers, were liberally
entertained by the aristocracy of the place, but unfortunately, they
were not Waterloo men.

Some time afterwards, while lying here, the supply of medals was
sent from London, with the names of the men they were intended for
engraved on the edge. On the distribution taking place, one of the
men, whose name was Hadly, a shoemaker, a native of Oxford, on
being called to receive his medal, I put a veto on his receiving it, by
informing the captain that the man was my rear-rank man, at Waterloo, and that he ran away to Brussels, and placing his arm in a sling,
reported himself wounded; suspicion was excited; he was examined,
and had not a scratch upon him. He was lodged in the guard-room,
and ordered to be marched a prisoner to his regiment; by some means
he had been transferred from one guard to another, and the crime
for which he had been detained, lost sight of. The captain, having
heard my statement, said he should withhold the medal, until the
circumstances could be inquired into. The man, ashamed to return to
his quarters without his medal, after having boasted of his presence
in the field of battle, deserted; he was quickly followed, taken at
Oxford among his friends, and was eventually sent to a condemned
regiment in Africa for life. A great many of the men were obliged
to return to their quarters without medals, and explained the circumstances, by stating that their names had been unfortunately omitted
in the list.

The latter end of May, 1816, our captain sent for me, and wished
(though it was not my turn for duty) that I should go on command,
with a deserter, to the Isle of Wight. I, of course, consented; and was
informed that the prisoner was a desperate character, and having a
great many acquaintances among the iron works, in the vicinity of
Wednesbury, through which we must pass, it was supposed they
would endeavour to rescue him. Next morning, having selected two
men to accompany me, and received each sixty rounds of ball
cartridges, the prisoner was given up to us, and having placed him
between the two men, with a strong pair of handcuffs upon him, I
walked behind. On the road we soon met some of the prisoner's
friends, who expressed themselves as follows—'Poor fellow; what a
shame to take him along handcuffed'; and as they increased in
numbers, and became very troublesome, wanting to treat the prisoner
with spirits, I allowed him to take some ale, with some whom he

stated to be related to him. At last, there appeared to be very evident symptoms of an endeavour to get him away.

As soon as I discovered this, I halted the party; and addressing the people, informed them that we had a duty to perform, and I hoped they would not interrupt us, as, it could not possibly do the prisoner any good, inasmuch as I should immediately shoot him, if they attempted to take him away by force. Finding this to be the case, (and a gentleman residing near there, coming by in his carriage stopping to point out to them the folly of their conduct), I was suffered to proceed, and got to Birmingham, in safety, when I lodged my prisoner in the prison for the night.

Calling for him, next morning, we proceeded by easy stages, stopping, at nights, at the following towns: Henly-upon-Arden, Stratford-upon-Avon, Shipston-on-Store [*Stour*], Woodstock, Oxford, Abington, Newbury, in Berkshire, Whitchurch, Winchester, to Southampton. The present destination of the prisoner was the large ship called the *Dido*, lying off the Isle of Wight, near Cowes.

The distance from Southampton to Cowes, is about fifteen miles. A man-of-war's boat happening to be near the shore at the time, they were ordered to take us over; but we had to wait about two hours, till they were ready, and finding they could not take the whole of us, I ordered my two men to get billets, and wait my return, the next day. I then fastened the prisoner's right hand to my left, with the handcuffs, and got into the boat. The tars had been drinking rather freely; and as soon as the sails were properly adjusted, measured their length at the bottom of the boat, except the man of the helm.

The wind was blowing very fresh, and a gentleman's yacht, on our starboard side, seemed anxious to get ahead of us: this, the coxswain of our boat by no means relished; and calling one of his men, they spread out every bit of canvas they had, and the boat cut through the water like a shot. The yacht also was put upon her metal, by the owner; and they made a very pretty race of it. I was afraid our boat would capsize, and took the precaution to release my own wrist from the handcuff, that I might have a chance of escape, if we should be immersed. The race was very strongly contested; but our boat beat by a quarter of a mile. Having taken in their sails, they rowed me to the prison-ship, and I surrendered my charge, and was not sorry for it.

While I was waiting on the quarter-deck of the ship, I saw a man on the main-deck whom I thought I knew; and yet, I could scarcely believe it possible that it could be the same. I enquired his name; they said it was Bryan; still I thought I was mistaken. I, however, requested leave to go on the main-deck among the prisoners, and coming suddenly behind the man I had been observing, I called out, 'Is that you, Dean?' he turned round, and said, 'Ah! Morris; is that you?' When we were lying at Courtray, in Belgium, this man was one of our drummers, and was confined in the guard-room for a crime which would have subjected him to corporal punishment. Some general visiting us at the time, we had a special parade ordered, and the colonel wishing the regiment to look as efficient and respectable as possible, ordered the prisoners from the guard-room, to take their places, intending that they should be again taken to the guard-room when the parade was over. After the regiment was dismissed, however, Drummer Dean was nowhere to be found: patrols were dispatched in every direction, but no tidings could be heard of him.

Next day, some of the inhabitants of the town brought his cap, greatcoat, sword, belt, and drum, which, according to their statement, had been found on the banks of the river Lys, which runs by the town. Some drags were procured, and some considerable time lost in searching for the body, there being not the slightest doubt of his having drowned himself, to avoid punishment. It was so reported to the authorities at home; and he thus prevented his name from appearing in the 'Hue and Cry' as a deserter, and he was enabled, by some means or other, to effect his escape from the country, and got back to his native place, in Ireland. Being an excellent scholar, he set up as schoolmaster, and got married to a decent young woman; but going to a neighbouring fair, he got drunk, and enlisted in a regiment then lying at Dublin. He had not been there more than a fortnight, when he deserted from them; was soon afterwards taken, tried by a court-martial, and ordered to be sent to a condemned regiment. He was now on board the *Dido*, waiting his turn to go.

After telling me the circumstances I have just narrated, he begged I would not mention it to the authorities on board, as it would add to his punishment.

On leaving the *Dido*, I had to take the receipt they had given me for the man's body, to the barracks, near Newport, to be counter-signed by the commanding officer there; and I slept at Newport that night. I rose early the next morning, walked to Cowes, obtained a passage by the king's boat to Southampton, joined my two men, and went back by the same easy stages we had come.

Our journey from Henly to Birmingham, was on the 18th of June, the first anniversary of the Battle of Waterloo. I intended to rejoice a little, as soon as my day's march was over, but on reaching Derritend, the entrance to the town, I was informed that the inhabitants had subscribed a sum of money to entertain the Waterloo men, in the barracks—two troops of the 15th Hussars; and the people got round me, and insisted that I also should go to the banquet. My companions had no medals; but they belonged to a Waterloo regiment, and that was sufficient; so having obtained billets, and deposited our arms and ammunition, we proceeded straight to the barracks, accompanied by two or three hundred people, who exclaimed, as we neared the barracks, 'Here, we've got some more Waterloo men!' and we were invited to join in the revelry.

In the space between the barrack-rooms and the riding-school, tables were spread, for the accommodation of the men. In the officers' mess-room, which was opposite, a grand dinner was provided, to which many of the gentry were invited; and both officers and men kept it up till a late hour. The way in which it was conducted was highly creditable to the subscribers, and the way in which it passed off was equally creditable to the recipients. It was late when I left; and I was then escorted by some parties, who insisted on going to my quarters, to take a parting glass.

Next morning we returned to Wolverhampton. Some few days afterwards, I had a very narrow escape from a violent death. I was sent for to quiet one of our men, who was drunk and disorderly in his quarters, the 'Pied Bull', in the road leading out to Dudley. On my entering the house, I found the man quarrelling with some colliers, and insisted upon his going to bed immediately, or else I threatened to send him to the guard-room. With the assistance of the landlord, his wife, and servant, I got the man upstairs, and placed him on his bed, when he took hold of his musket, which was close by, and deliberately putting the muzzle to my breast, said, 'D——n you; I'll shoot you!' Not supposing the piece to be loaded, I gently removed it from my breast, when it exploded—the ball passing between my arm and my side, lodged in the wall, over the window, where, probably, it still remains.

As I was acquainted with the man's friends, who were respectable tradespeople in Birmingham, I did not confine him, as the punishment, under such circumstances, would have been very severe; but I borrowed a stick from the landlord, and I laboured on him till he fairly cried, and then went to sleep.

One of our companies, from Nottingham, being sent to do duty at Birmingham, I was ordered to join them. This company was commanded by the officer, whom I have already introduced to the reader, as General Crawford. What became of him during the Battle of Waterloo, I never could learn, but he was not with us; he had now again dwindled down to a simple captain.

There happened at this time rather a serious riot in Birmingham, owing to the prevailing distress of the people, many of whom, who, to my knowledge, had been in the habit of earning two and three pounds a week, were then reduced to the necessity of sweeping the streets, for a shilling a day, and the riot was produced by a tradesman, who had the superintendence of some relief fund, saying that seven shillings per week, was enough for a man and his family to subsist on. The first operation of the mob, was the demolition of his house and furniture.

The two troops of the 15th Hussars were in the barracks, and my company was scattered over the town, in quarters. As soon as I heard of the riot, I went round, collected our men, and took them to the captain's quarters, who complimented me for my alacrity in getting the men together. The idea of having an opportunity of contending with a mob, seemed most congenial to his sentiments. He took us first to the barrack, for a supply of ball-cartridge, from the magazine there, and then led us into the town, where the number of rioters had increased to some thousands, and mischief was expected from them. The high constable went with us, and proceeded to read the riot act. On some brickbats and stones being thrown at us, our brave captain gave orders to load, and he then gave direction that we should fire among the mob, when the high constable interposed, and said, 'There was no necessity for that yet.' 'Then,' said our officer, 'if I am not allowed to fire, I shall take my men back!' The constable's patriotic answer deserves to be recorded, 'Sir,' said he, 'you are called on to aid and assist the civil power, and if you fire on the people, without my permission, and death ensues, you will be guilty of murder, and if you go away, without my leave, it will be at your peril.' The officer seemed nettled at the circumstance, but consoled himself with the thought, that we should even yet have the privilege of killing a few people.

About midnight, the rioters retired to their homes; we were patrolling the streets, with the two troops of Hussars, and took a few prisoners, whom we conveyed to the prison in Moor Street. Next morning, the rioters assembled in large numbers, and the general of the district arriving, special constables were sworn, and dispatches sent off for more troops. After the special constables had been mustered and armed, with staves or staffs, we made a dart at the rioters, and secured about twenty or thirty of the most violent, who were immediately taken before a magistrate and committed to Warwick gaol.

That the mob contemplated something serious, there was no doubt, as a good many iron balls were found in the streets, having spikes in them, to cripple the horses of the Hussars.

The mob, finding such efficient measures taken against them, began gradually to disperse, and though it was considered advisable to patrol the streets again during the night, there was no more disturbance; and next day, the ebullition subsided, without the loss of life. Had we fired on the people in the first instance, the consequences must have been dreadful.

The male population of Birmingham contains a greater number of old soldiers than any other town in the kingdom, and in war time they furnished double the quantity of recruits of any town in the kingdom; and though they might not have taken part in the riot, there can be no doubt that they would have assisted in taking revenge, for an uncalled-for and wanton attack on the lives of their townsmen. Our officer was so pleased with my conduct during this affair, that he made a special report of it, and it was inserted in the orderly book of the regiment.

At this time, one of the men obtained a pass, to visit his friends, a few miles distant; and as he became the hero of an incident of a somewhat interesting nature, I shall take the liberty of giving a sketch of his early history, as related to me by himself, when we were on watch together, and pacing the deck of a vessel, one dark cold night, in November, 1813, crossing the German Ocean, and going with a stiff breeze, at the rate of nine or ten knots an hour.

The father of Richard Barton, had for many years, occupied a small farm, about midway between the towns of Stafford and Litchfield; and though they had at no time been rich, they had borne an irreproachable character for honesty, industry, and sobriety, and by the practice of those virtues, they had hitherto managed to keep the 'wolf from the door'. The only child they had left, was the subject of these remarks; who, as he grew up towards manhood, assisted his father in the management of their farm. At length, it was their lot to meet some reverses, which led to the breaking-up of their once happy home, and drove the young Richard to the adoption of a military life.

Several consecutive bad crops, together with the depression in the market, and a long and painful illness, to which the old man was subjected, threw their affairs into irremediable confusion. The arrears of rent were demanded, by an inexorable landlord; who, on finding them unable to pay, at once despoiled them of all their little property, and drove them forth destitute and friendless.

As soon as Richard had obtained a temporary shelter for his parents, in a small cottage, he left them, with the view of obtaining some sort of employment, whereby he might be enabled to support them. On entering the town of Stafford, he was met by a recruiting sergeant, who strove to enlist him by the offer of the ordinary bounty then given. Failing in this, and pleased with Richard's manly appearance, he informed him that he had instructions to provide a substitute for a young opulent farmer, who had been drawn into the Staffordshire militia, and who would give fifty pounds for an able substitute. This large offer, opening to the young man the means of rendering relief to his parents, was accepted. He was sworn in, and on receiving his bounty, retaining only so much as was necessary for his equipment, he forwarded the rest to his parents.

On his joining the regiment, at Windsor, he received a further bounty of fourteen pounds, to volunteer into the line, ten of which, also he forwarded to his parents. However acceptable these sums of money might be to the old couple in their destitute condition, it was with the utmost reluctance they could be induced to use them, considering it as the blood-money of their only child; and when compelled eventually to make use of it, they determined to retain only the interest or profit upon it, so that the capital might be available in purchasing their son's discharge, on his return to England.

The old man having regained his health, embarked in some farming speculations, which proved successful; and by the death of a relative soon afterwards, he received such an accession of funds, as enabled him to become the proprietor of a very respectable roadside country inn; and all that was now wanted to make them happy, was the safe return of their 'dear boy'.

Young Richard, in the meantime, was knocking about with us, on the Continent. He was fortunately one of the few survivors in the Battle of Waterloo; and, on our return to England, and approaching his native county, he was anxious, once more, to see his parents; and with this view, as I have already stated, he had obtained a pass.

On the very day he was journeying homeward, his parents, hearing of the arrival of the regiment in their vicinity, had left home, to see him. On Richard's arrival at the house of his parents, he was made acquainted with their journey, and its object; and as they could not return till the next day, being fatigued with his march, he obtained some refreshment, and went early to bed, without acquainting the two servant girls of his relationship to their master.

As soon as the old couple had started on their journey, the ostler connected with the establishment, left the house, ostensibly to pass the evening with some companions in the neighbouring village; and, as he had not returned at the usual hour for closing the house, they fastened the doors, and anxiously awaited his arrival.

About one o'clock in the morning, they were much alarmed at a strange noise in the house, and their suspicion was excited, that the soldier, taking advantage of the loneliness of their situation, was in the act of plundering the premises. Having mustered up sufficient courage to visit his apartment, they found him asleep. They awoke him, and explained the circumstance which induced them to do so. He desired them to retire, while he dressed himself; and having done so, he preceded them down stairs, with his musket loaded and the bayonet fixed.

On going down, they saw a light and heard some voices proceeding from the bar-parlour, and, on throwing open the door, three men were discovered, one of whom the girls recognised as the ostler, though he, as well as the confederates, had blackened their faces. On being thus detected, they armed themselves with knives, but, as the only means of egress was by the door—the shutters being securely fastened, and the soldier having stationed himself in the doorway, and expressed his determination of shooting the first man that attempted to stir,—he managed to keep them at bay, until the girls, whom he sent for assistance, returned with the constables, and the prisoners were strongly secured with handcuffs, and conveyed to the cage.

The next day, at noon, the old people returned, and had the happiness, not only to meet their dear son, but to find also, that he had been the means, under Providence, of saving their property, from the grasp of the midnight robber. As the Assizes were close at hand, and as the soldier was the principal witness, his leave of absence was extended. On the trial of the offenders, their guilt being clearly established, they were severally transported for life.

In the meantime, the necessary means had been taken to purchase the soldier's discharge: and on his marrying a farmer's daughter, in the neighbourhood, the old people resigned to them the management of the inn, which they conducted for many years, with advantage, respected by all who knew them; and there were few persons in the district, who did not feel a sort of pleasure in relating the circumstances attending the Soldier's Return.

About a month after this, our regiment was removed again, the headquarters being at Chelmsford, and two companies ordered to do duty at Yarmouth. I was detached on this duty, under the command of a Captain Chislem. Our road lay through Newport Pagnel and Cambridge. After leaving the latter place, and while on the line of march, a gentleman rode after us, and reported the loss of some silver spoons, which he suspected had been taken by the man, who had been quartered on him. The man, Jeremiah Bates, was searched, and the spoons found in his knapsack. They were restored to the owner. This was the man who had accidentally shot the officer [*Lieutenant Strachan*] at Quatre Bras, on the morning of the 17th of June.

Our last stage was from Norwich to Yarmouth, and for the expedition and novelty of the thing, we were to go by a steam-boat; but when morning came, it being Sunday, such a number had paid for a trip by the steamer, that we could not be accommodated, and were therefore obliged to walk the distance of eighteen miles. We were not sorry for the disappointment next day, when he learned that the boiler of the steamer had burst, and numbers of persons had been mutilated.

We remained at Yarmouth several months, in the hospital on the Danes, which was converted into barracks for our use, and very pretty, comfortable barracks they were, but very cold in winter.

Excepting furnishing two small guards, we had no parade or other duty to perform here, and the captain was a good sort of fellow; indeed, too much so, for he mixed in so much society, that he overrun the constable, and his own pay being insufficient for him, and being disappointed in a supply of money from his friends, at Derby, he made free with the company's funds.

On the shore at Yarmouth, called the Danes (from the circumstance of the Danes having landed there, when they invaded this country), there was the South Star Battery, of which we furnished the guard of twelve men; and an artillery man had charge of the cannon.

One night I was the sergeant of this guard, and was informed that a number of smugglers were then landing their contraband cargo, and the artillery man insisted that it was my duty to capture them. Accordingly, I went with ten men, leaving two on sentry. The night was very dark and cold, in the month of February, and as we went towards the sea, we could perceive, between us and the water, a body of men moving about; on coming near them, one of the party advanced, and said, 'I'll tell you what, gentlemen, you had better have nothing to do with us. We know how many there are of you, and though you have muskets, you have no ammunition (which was the fact), now we have got some bull-dogs (pistols) here, which you won't much relish. So take my advice, go back, and if you stumble over a keg, take it with you.'

As I found I should really have no chance in contending with them in the dark, we took the advice, and returned to the fort; and I then found the men had actually brought with them a keg of hollands, containing about a couple of gallons, which they made so free with during the night, that when the new guard came next day, my men were in such a state, that I could not think of taking them home with me; so I left them asleep on the guard-bed, and left directions for them to return to the barracks separately, so as not to be observed.

It was my duty, on returning to the barracks, to go to the room of the officer of the day, and report that I had brought such a guard home; and his duty was to inspect them, and if they were all right, to dismiss them.

I had no guard with me, but I went to the officer's room (he is now a major in the service, and, therefore, I must not mention his name). It was well known, at the time, that he was rather too intimate with his servant's wife, and she was in his room when I knocked. He called, 'Who's there?' I replied, that I had brought the South Star Guard home. 'Oh!' said he, 'are they all right?' 'Yes, Sir.' 'Well; dismiss them.' And I went to my room, glad that I had got over that scrape so easily.

In the month of May, 1817, the out-companies were called in to Chelmsford, and orders came for the reduction of the 2nd battalion; the men, such as were serviceable, to be sent to the 1st battalion, in the East Indies, at the Island of Ceylon.

On the appointed day for breaking up our battalion, after parade, the major formed us into a square, and after a very impressive speech, in reference to our past services, the order for the disbandment was read, the colours, under which we had fought so often, were taken from their staff (the men presenting arms during the ceremony) and carefully placed in a box, and afterwards forwarded to London. There was scarcely a man among us, who did not shed a tear at the separation. Three hundred and eleven men were sent to the Indies, among whom was my brother, who received the appointment of armourer, and remained five years at Ceylon, during which the regiment suffered much from the cholera morbus, and other diseases incidental to the climate.

On the return of my brother to England, he was apparently worn out, so that they pensioned him off; but a few months' residence at home restored his health, and he accepted another appointment, as armourer of the 63rd, and joined them at Hobart Town, Van Dieman's Land, where he remained six years. From thence they went to Fort George, where they stopped three years, then went a considerable distance through the interior of India, where the regiment still remains, and my brother has left three of his eldest children with them. He, however, came home again, and appeared quite an old man. He was again pensioned off, received an additional allowance for his extra service, making in the whole twenty-five years. Though so emaciated when he came home, such is the natural strength of his constitution, that in a few months he became as well as ever he was, and his first wife having died on the passage from Van Dieman's Land to India, he has now not only another wife, but also another child.

When our battalion was reduced, I was sent with a recruiting-party, to Birmingham; and the first day I beat-up through the town, I was so fortunate as to get sixteen recruits, which I thought a pretty good day's work; but on taking them before the major, next morning, he laughed at me, and let me into the secret, that out of the sixteen I had enlisted, and on whom I had already spent about three pounds, there was not one fit for service, each of them being about half or three quarters of an inch too short.

I went back to my rendezvous, the 'Coach and Horses', in the Bull-ring, and began to consider how I should wipe out the disgrace of having been so easily duped. I soon hit upon a plan, which I thought would answer my purpose. I wrote a letter, and signed it with a fictitious commanding officer's name, authorising me to enlist men for 'general service', for which I might take them one inch below the standard. I went immediately to the major, and he very much approved of the plan, as the young men had given him a great deal of trouble, enlisting, and being brought before him by every fresh party who entered the town. A summons was therefore issued, officially, by him, informing them of my special instruction to enlist for general service; they were thunder-struck at the circumstance, and I was beset by their relatives, begging to be let off. As my object was to punish them, and get my own money back, I agreed to release them, by the payment of such sums, as I thought their circumstances would allow, and they were so ashamed of the affair, that they never again troubled the recruiting parties, but when we went through the town afterwards, it was said, 'Here comes the general service party.'

On my return, from this duty, to the depot, at Chelmsford, I was particularly urged by the officer in command, to extend my time of service, and join the regiment in India; but I refused, being disappointed in the nature of the service, and having no desire to wear away the best portion of my existence in a subordinate capacity, where the chances of promotion were so precarious, and the reward, as last, so trifling. Having only enlisted for seven years, which were drawing to a close, the government sent down my discharge to Chelmsford. Captain Cohen, who commanded the depot at the time, filled it up and gave me an extraordinary good character; and was so sorry to part with me, that he sent a sergeant after me, who overtook me at Ingatestone. His instructions were to treat me liberally, to talk over our battles and to endeavour, if possible, to enlist me again.

I could see through the sergeant's intention, which was to get me in a state of intoxication, and then to entrap me. But I turned the tables on him most effectually. I drank freely with him, but stood it better than he did; so having fairly knocked him up and had him put to bed, I mounted the first stage that came by, and returned home to London, and soon, unassisted attained a respectable position in civil society; and I have the satisfaction to reflect that I have served my country faithfully and efficiently, during a portion of the most eventful period of its history, without putting it to any expense, beyond my mere pay while serving. If these recollections should afford any amusement, instruction, or information and if the publication of them should yield a trifle over the expenses of printing, etc, I shall consider myself amply repaid for my trouble; and I now, most respectfully, bid my readers   FAREWELL!

Appendix I

Historical Record of the Second Battalion of the Seventy-Third Regiment[1]

Europe enjoyed but a short interval of tranquillity by the treaty of Amiens, which was signed on 27 March, 1802. In May of the following year, the war was renewed, and Napoleon Bonaparte, the First Consul of the French Republic, threatened the invasion of Great Britain. On 18 May, 1804, Napoleon was invested with the dignity of Emperor of the French, and on 26 May of the succeeding year, he was crowned at Milan as King of Italy.

In December, 1804, Spain issued a declaration of war against England, and agreed to furnish a powerful aid to the French Emperor.

While the French pursued a victorious career in Germany, they experienced dreadful reverses from the British navy, particularly on 21 October, 1805, when the combined fleets of France and Spain were completely defeated off Cape Trafalgar. The victory was, however, clouded by the death of Admiral Viscount Nelson, to whose memory a grateful and admiring nation paid the highest honours.

In the year 1806, the Seventy-Third regiment arrived in England from the East Indies, and two years afterwards was ordered to embark for New South Wales. On the promulgation of the orders for this embarkation, it was directed that a *second battalion* should be added to the regiment, which was to be placed on the establishment of the army from 24 December, 1808.

The second battalion was, in the first instance, to consist of four companies, at a hundred rank and file each; upon the effectives exceeding four hundred, it was to be augmented to six hundred, which number being completed, it was to be augmented to a thousand rank and file.

The battalion was embodied at Nottingham and was considerably strengthened, within the year 1809, by volunteers from the English, Irish, and Scotch Militia.

In March, 1810, the battalion proceeded to Ashborne, and subsequently to Derby and Ashford.

[1] From Cannon's *History of the 73rd Regiment.*

On 25 October, 1811, the establishment of the battalion was augmented to six companies, consisting of thirty-four sergeants, twelve drummers, and six hundred rank and file.

In July, 1812, the battalion was removed from Ashford to Deal, and afterwards proceeded to the Tower of London.

While quartered in the Tower of London, in 1813, the battalion was augmented to ten companies, consisting of forty-five sergeants, twenty-two drummers, and eight hundred rank and file. The battalion proceeded to Colchester in April.

The dreadful disasters experienced by the French in their retreat from Russia, combined with the successes obtained over the forces of Napoleon in the Peninsula by the allies under the Marquis of Wellington, caused the separation of Prussia and other states from the interest of France, and a treaty of alliance and subsidy was concluded between Great Britain and Sweden, in which it was stipulated that a Swedish army, commanded by the Crown Prince, should join the Allies.

On 25 May, 1813, the battalion, under the command of Lieut.-Colonel William George (afterwards Lord) Harris, embarked on a particular service at Harwich, but subsequently joined the expedition to Stralsund, in Swedish Pomerania, under the command of Major-General Samuel Gibbs, and landed at that town on 7 August.

From Stralsund the Seventy-Third proceeded to join the allied forces under the command of Lieut.-General Count Walmoden, who engaged, and completely defeated, the enemy on the plains of Gorde, on 16 September, 1813. The Seventy-Third was the only British battalion in the action.[1]

The battalion was afterwards ordered to join the British forces,

---

[1] The following statement of the above operations is contained in the *Annual Register*, vol. 87, page 280: 'After landing at Stralsund, and assisting in completing the works of that town, Lieut.-Colonel Harris, with the Seventy-Third, was detached into the interior of the country, to feel for the enemy, and also to get into communication with Lieut.-General Count Walmoden, which dangerous service he successfully effected, though he had, with great care and caution, to creep with his small force between the large *corps d'armée* of Davout and other French generals at that time stationed in Pomerania, Mecklenburg, and Hanover. Having joined Count Walmoden, the Seventy-Third contributed greatly to the victory that General gained over the French on the plains of Gorde, in Hanover, where Lieut.-Colonel Harris, at the head of his battalion, declining any aid, and at the moment when the German hussars had been routed, charged up a steep hill, took a battery of French artillery, and unfurling the British colours, at once spread terror amongst that gallant enemy which feared no others; a panic struck them, and they fled.'

then in the north of Germany, under the command of Major-General Samuel Gibbs, at Rostock, and subsequently embarked for England at Warnemunde, on 2 November, but on arriving at Yarmouth the battalion was ordered, without landing, to join the army in Holland under General Sir Thomas Graham, afterwards Lord Lynedoch: the battalion arrived at Williamstadt on 18 December.

The Prussian General, Bülow, having requested that the British would make a forward movement upon Antwerp, to favour his operations, the battalion accordingly marched to the attack of that place, which was bombarded by the British forces on 13 January, 1814; and again from 2 until 6 February, for the purpose of destroying the French fleet lying there.

In the attack on the village of Merxem on 2 February, 1814, where the enemy was strongly posted, Lieutenant John McConnell, and Lieutenant and Adjutant Thomas Frederick James were wounded, the former severely. A volunteer, named J. Simpson, was also dangerously wounded. This youth was about sixteen years of age, and was attached to the light company. Soon after the action commenced, and in the course of a few minutes, he was shot through both legs, before which a bullet had lodged in the butt of his firelock. His military career was short, as he died of his wounds in a few days.

On this occasion, the light company, under Captain Richard Drewe, supported the ninety-fifth (rifle brigade) in driving the enemy from the *abatis* formed at the entrance to the village. The troops suffered very severely during the foregoing operations from the intense cold, the winter being unusually severe, and though sleeping on the line of march was generally fatal, it was no easy matter to prevent it.

General Sir Thomas Graham stated in his despatch, 'All the troops engaged behaved with the usual spirit and intrepidity of British soldiers, and the conduct of Major Dawson Kelly, of the Seventy-Third, was particularly noticed'.

After this success the British troops were employed in constructing a breastwork and battery; on 3 February several pieces of heavy ordnance opened upon the city of Antwerp, and on the French shipping in the Scheldt; the cannonade was continued until the 6th, when General Bülow, having receive orders to march southward, to act with the grand army of the Allies, it became necessary to relinquish the attack on Antwerp, when the British retired towards Breda.

On 16 March, 1814, a detachment of the Seventy-Third, consisting of 200 men, under the command of Major Dawson Kelly, was bombarded by a French seventy-four gun ship and eight gun brigs, in Fort Frederick on the river Scheldt.

Peace was shortly afterwards concluded. On 4 April, Napoleon Bonaparte signed his abdication in favour of his son; but this proposal being rejected, he signed in a few days a second abdication, renouncing the thrones of France and Italy entirely for himself and heirs. He afterwards selected Elba for his residence, which island was ceded to him in full sovereignty for life, and a pension payable from the revenues of France, and by the treaty which was signed at Paris on 11 April between the Allies and Napoleon, it was agreed that he should enjoy the imperial title for life. Ample pensions were also assigned to his relatives.

On 3 May, 1814, Louis XVIII entered Paris, and ascended the throne of his ancestors, and on the 30th of that month the general peace between France and the allied powers of Austria, Russia, Great Britain and Prussia, was signed at Paris.

In the beginning of May, the battalion was ordered into quarters at Antwerp, and in September following it marched to Tournay, where it arrived in October.

The commencement of the year 1815 saw Louis XVIII apparently firmly seated on the throne of France; but various causes of discontent existed in that country. The army, long accustomed to war, still retained a chivalrous veneration for Napoleon Bonaparte, who was kept acquainted with the state of the public mind, and this feeling of his former troops. In the evening of 26 February he embarked at Porto Ferrajo, in the Island of Elba, with about a thousand troops, of whom a few were French, and the remainder Poles, Corsicans, Neapolitans, and Elbese. With this motley band he landed at Cannes, in Provence, on 1 March, 1815, and the result proved that his calculations were correct. After being joined by the garrison of Grenoble, he proceeded to Lyons, and entered that city amidst the acclamation of 'Vive l'Empereur!' from the soldiers and the people. The possession of the second city in France being thus obtained, Napoleon assumed his former dignity of Emperor, and continued his advance to Paris, which he reached on 20 March, his progress having been a continued triumph.

In the meantime, Louis XVIII had withdrawn from Paris to Ghent, and Napoleon took possession of the throne of France as Emperor, but the allied powers refused to acknowledge his sovereignty, and determined to effect his dethronement.

The battalion had remained stationed between Tournay and Courtray until March, 1815, when, in consequence of the foregoing events, it was ordered to join the division of the army under the command of Lieut.-General Baron Alten, and formed part of the brigade of Major-General Sir Colin Halkett, KCB.

On 11 April, 1815, it was announced to the army in Flanders that His Royal Highness the Prince Regent, in the name and behalf of His Majesty, had appointed Field Marshal the Duke of Wellington, KG, to be commander of His Majesty's forces on the continent of Europe, and it was directed that the Fifth British brigade of infantry should be composed of the second battalion of the thirtieth, the thirty-third, and the second battalions of the sixty-ninth and seventy-third regiments.

Napoleon left Paris on 12 June, and endeavoured, by one of those rapid and decisive movements for which he had been celebrated, to interpose his forces between the British and Prussian armies, and then attack them in detail. Information of this movement arrived at Brussels during the evening of 15 June, and the troops were immediately ordered to prepare to march.

On the 16 June, the division of which the second battalion of the Seventy-Third formed part, pursued its course, with the other portions of the army, through the forest of Soignies, Genappe, and along the road towards Charleroi. After a march of twenty two miles the troops arrived at the post of Les Quatre Bras, where the second French corps, under Marshal Ney, was developing a serious attack against that position, with very superior numbers.

As the British regiments arrived at the scene of conflict, they were instantly formed for action. The repeated charges of the French were repulsed, but a considerable loss was incurred, including his Serene Highness the Duke of Brunswick, who fell at the head of his troops.

The Seventy-Third had the following officers wounded: Lieutenants John Acres and John Lloyd, and Ensigns Robert Greville Heselrige and Thomas Deacon.[1] Lieutenant Acres died of his wounds. One drummer, and three rank and file were killed, and one sergeant and forty-three rank and file wounded.

Marshal Blücher had been attacked on 16 June by Napoleon at

---

[1] Morris's company.

Ligny, and the Prussians, after a desperate conflict, were compelled to retreat to Wavre. This caused the Duke of Wellington to make a corresponding movement, to keep up his communication with them.

In the course of the morning of 17 June, the troops were withdrawn from Quatre Bras, and proceeded towards Waterloo. On this day, the Seventy-Third had Lieutenant Joseph William Henry Streaphan [*Strachan*][1] and three rank and file killed.

The position which the Duke of Wellington occupied in front of Waterloo crossed the high roads leading from Charleroi and Nivelle to Brussels, and which roads united at the village of Mont St Jean, in the rear of the British. The right wing extended to a ravine near Merbe Braine, which was occupied. The left extended to a height above the hamlet of Ter la Haye, which was likewise occupied. In front of the right centre, and near the Nivelle road, the house and garden of Hougonmont were taken possession of, and in front of the left centre, the farm of La Haye Sainte was occupied. By the left the British communicated with Marshal Prince Blücher at Wavre, through Ohain.

Napoleon collected his army on a range of heights in front of the British, with the exception of his third corps, which he had sent to observe the Prussians. About ten o'clock the French commenced a furious attack upon the post at Hougonmont. Then ensued a conflict which will ever be memorable in the history of Europe. The attacks of the French troops were frequently calculated to spread confusion through any army. They were supported by the thunder of a numerous artillery, and followed up by such a succession of column after column, rolling onwards like the waves of the sea, that it required a degree of unexampled fortitude and courage to oppose effectual resistance to so fierce and continued a storm of war.

That degree of courage was not wanting in the British ranks, and paralysed by the fierce determination of his opponents, the attacks of Napoleon's legions relaxed; the Prussians arrived on the left; to co-operate the Anglo-Belgian army formed line, and with one impetuous charge decided the fortune of the day. The French were driven from the field with the loss of their cannon and equipage, and the hopes of Bonaparte were annihilated.

During the greater part of the battle, the Seventy-Third, with the second battalion of the thirtieth, were very much exposed to the

---

[1] Morris's company.

enemy's artillery, and constantly engaged in repelling numerous charges of cavalry that appeared determined to break their square, which ultimately was reduced to a very small size, from the casualties occasioned by round and grap shot. Lieutenant Robert Stewart [*the junior Lieutenant*], one of the junior officers of the Seventy-Third, commanded the battalion at the termination of the battle, and in consequence was some years afterwards promoted to a company without purchase.[1]

The casualties amongst the officers were unusually great. Of twenty-three who marched into action on 16 June at Quatre Bras, twenty-two were killed and wounded on that and the two following days.

In the battle on 18 June the Seventy-Third had Captains Alexander Robertson[2] and John Kennedy; Lieutenant Matthew Hollis; and Ensigns William Law[*son*] Lowe and Charles Page killed.

The officers wounded were Lieut.-Colonel William George Harris (Colonel) commanding the battalion, severely; Major Archibald John Maclean, who died of his wounds: Captains Henry Coane, William Wharton and John Garland, all severely. Lieutenants John McConnell, Thomas Reynolds, and Donald Browne all severely; Lieutenant Browne afterwards died of his wounds. Ensigns William McBean, Charles Bedford Eastwood, and George Dandridge Bridge (severely) and Ensign and Adjutant Patrick Hay severely.

Three sergeants, one drummer, and forty-three rank and file were killed, and thirteen sergeants, two drummers, and one hundred and sixty rank and file were wounded; twenty-four of the above number died of their wounds; forty-one rank and file were missing.

In acknowledgement of the services which the army performed in the battle of Waterloo, and the actions immediately preceding it, each subaltern officer and soldier present were permitted to count two years' additional service, and silver medals were conferred on all ranks, bearing on the one side an impression of His Royal Highness

[1] 'Once, and once only, during the dreadful carnage at Waterloo, did the stern Seventy-Third hesitate to fill up a gap which the relentless iron had torn in their square; their Lieut.-Colonel (Brevet-Colonel Harris) at once pushing his horse lengthwise across the space, said with a smile, "Well, my lads, if you won't, I must"; it is almost needless to add that immediately he was led back to his proper place, and the ranks closed up by men still more devoted than before' (*Annual Register*, vol. 87, page 280). A similar account is given in Dalton's *Waterloo Roll Call.*

[2] Clearly Morris's company commander.

the Prince Regent, and on the reverse the figure of Victory, holding the palm in the right hand, and the olive branch in the left, with the word 'Wellington' over its head, and 'WATERLOO', 18th June, 1815, at its feet.

The thanks of both Houses of Parliament were voted to the army with the greatest enthusiasm, 'for its distinguished valour at Waterloo'; and the Seventy-Third and other regiments engaged, were permitted to bear the word 'WATERLOO' on their colours and appointments, in commemoration of their distinguished services on 18 June, 1815.

After the battle of Waterloo, the battalion, which was reduced to a complete skeleton, advanced with the army to Paris, where it arrived in the first week in July, and encamped in the Bois de Boulogne until November, when it was placed in cantonments in the vicinity of that metropolis.

Meanwhile Louis XVIII had entered Paris, and was again reinstated on the throne of his ancestors. Napoleon Bonaparte had surrendered himself to Captain Maitland, commanding the *Bellerophon* British ship of war, and the island of St Helena having been fixed for his residence, he was conveyed thither, with a few of his zealous adherents.

When the allied forces retired from Paris in December, 1815, with the exception of the 'Army of Occupation' left in France, the second battalion of the Seventy-Third regiment was ordered to return to England; it embarked at Calais on 23 December, and landed on the same day at Ramsgate; from Ramsgate it marched to Colchester to join the depot, which continued in that town during the absence of the battalion on foreign service.

The battalion afterwards marched to Nottingham, where it arrived on 12 February, 1816.

The battalion was stationed between Nottingham, Weedon, and Colchester, until May, 1817, when it was ordered to proceed to Chelmsford to be disbanded, which measure took place on 4 May, 1817, the most effective men, consisting of three hundred and ten non-commissioned officers and privates being embarked to join the first battalion of the regiment at Ceylon.

CONCLUSION

The earlier services of the Seventy-Third regiment, originally formed as a second battalion to the forty-second Highlanders, are connected with the wars against Hyder Ali and his son, Tippoo Saib, the powerful sultans of the Mysore territory: the word *'Mangalore'* granted by royal authority for the gallant defence of that fortress in 1783, and the word *'Seringapatam'* for the share taken by the regiment in the capture of the capital of Tippoo's country in 1799, when that sovereign terminated his career by a soldier's death, are borne on the regimental colour and appointments in commemoration of these arduous campaigns in India.

Other services were, however, performed by the regiment in the East, among which may be named the capture of the French settlement of Pondicherry in 1793, and that of the Dutch island of Ceylon in 1796, when the French Directory had caused Holland to become involved in hostilities with Great Britain.

After a service of twenty-four years in India, the regiment returned to England, and arrived at Greenwich in July, 1806.

In 1809 the regiment proceeded to New South Wales, when a second battalion was added to its establishment.

Brief as was the career of the second battalion, namely from 1809 to 1817, it added the imperishable word 'WATERLOO' to the regimental colour and appointments, that distinction being conferred by the Sovereign to commemorate its services in that battle, which gave a lengthened peace to the powers of Europe.

In 1814 the first battalion embarked from New South Wales for Ceylon, in the capture of which island the regiment had formerly participated.

The regiment returned to England in 1821, and continued on home service until 1827, when it embarked for Gibraltar, from which fortress it proceeded to Malta in 1829, and in 1834 to the Ionian Islands, whence it returned to Gibraltar in 1838, and embarked for North America.

In 1841 the regiment returned to England, and, in 1845, proceeded to the Cape of Good Hope, where it is now employed in active operations against the Kaffirs.

The orderly behaviour of the regiment in quarters, whether employed at home, or on foreign stations, combined with its soldier-like conduct in the field, have secured the confidence of the nation, and the approbation of the Sovereign.

1851

Appendix II
William George Lord Harris[1]

This distinguished officer was the son of General the first Lord Harris, and entered the army as an ensign in the seventy-sixth regiment of infantry, on 24 May, 1795; was promoted lieutenant in the thirty-sixth regiment on 3 January, 1796, from which he was removed to the seventy-fourth Highlanders on 4 September following, and joined in India in 1797. Lieutenant Harris served at the battle of Mallavelly on 27 March, 1799, and during the campaign under his father, Lord Harris, which led to the capture of Seringapatam, and was in nearly all the affairs, out-posts, and in the storming party on 4 May, 1799, which carried that fortress, where Lieutenant Harris was one of the first to enter the breach, for which he was commended on the spot by Major-General (afterwards Sir David) Baird. Being sent home with the captured standards, Lieutenant Harris had the honor of presenting them to His Majesty King George III, and was promoted to a company in the forty-ninth regiment, on 16 October, 1800, which he joined at Jersey, and embarking with it towards the end of the year for England, was wrecked on the passage off Guernsey. Captain Harris afterwards accompanied his regiment in the expedition to the Baltic under the command of Admiral Parker and Viscount Nelson and was present in the *Glatton* frigate in the desperate action off Copenhagen on 2 April, 1801. In 1802, Captain Harris embarked with the forty-ninth regiment for Canada, and served in the upper province for two years; being then appointed to a majority in the Seventy-Third regiment, he proceeded to join that corps in India, and on his way out was employed at the capture of the Cape of Good Hope in January, 1806, and was present at the action of Blue Berg. The Seventy-Third having quitted India previously to his arrival, he returned to England the same year, and found he had succeeded to the lieut.-colonelcy of that regiment. Upon the formation of the second battalion of the Seventy-Third, which was placed on the establishment of the army from 24 December, 1808, Lieut-Colonel Harris

[1] From Cannon's *History of the 73rd Regiment*.

was appointed to the command of it, and zealously applied himself to perfecting its discipline, and rendering it efficient in every respect. In 1813, Lieut.-Colonel Harris embarked on a particular service with the second battalion of the Seventy-Third regiment, but afterwards joined the expedition to Stralsund, in Swedish Pomerania, under Major-General Samuel Gibbs. On arrival Lieut.-Colonel Harris was selected to take the field with his battalion, and place himself under the orders of Lieut.-General Count Walmoden, and was present in the action of the Gorde (in which he highly distinguished himself), under that commander, on 16 September, 1813. In November, 1813, the second battalion of the Seventy-Third re-embarked in the Gulf of Lubec for England; but on arriving at Yarmouth, it was ordered, without landing, to join the army of General Sir Thomas Graham (afterwards Lord Lynedoch) in Holland. During the winter campaign before Antwerp, rendered more difficult in consequence of the severity of the weather, Lieut.-Colonel Harris had the honor of carrying the village of Merxem by storm, under the eye of His late Majesty King William IV, then Duke of Clarence, and, during the remainder of the operations, was employed as brigadier-general. After the peace of 1814, when Antwerp was delivered up, Colonel Harris, to which rank he had been promoted on 4 June, 1814, was quartered in that town, and remained in the Low Countries with his battalion during the remainder of the year 1814, and the early part of 1815. On the return of Napoleon from Elba, Colonel Harris joined the army of the Duke of Wellington, and his battalion was appointed to the brigade commanded by Major-General Sir Colin Halkett, and took part in the stubborn contest of 16 June, 1815, at Quatre Bras,—assisted in covering the retreat on the 17th; and on 18 June, at Waterloo, bore a gallant part in the complete defeat of Napoleon in that memorable battle. Colonel Harris, late in the afternoon, received a shot through the right shoulder, from which severe wound he continued to suffer at times for the remainder of his life. On retiring on half pay, a testimony of admiration and regard was presented to him by the officers of his battalion in the shape of a splendid sword. On 19 July, 1821, Colonel Harris was advanced to the rank of Major-General. Major-General the Honourable William George Harris was employed on the staff of the army in Ireland from 17 May, 1823, until 24 June, 1825, when he was appointed to the command of the northern district of Great Britain, which he retained until 24 July, 1828, and contributed materially in quelling the disturbances in the manufacturing districts.

On the decease of his father, Lord Harris, in 1829, he succeeded to the title, and from that period lived in retirement at Belmont, the family seat, near Faversham in Kent. On 3 December, 1832, Major-General Lord Harris was appointed colonel of the eighty-sixth regiment, and was removed to the Seventy-Third on 4 December, 1835. In January, 1837, Lord Harris was promoted to the rank of Lieut.-General. His decease occurred at Belmont, after a short illness, on 30 May, 1845. Lord Harris was a Knight Commander of the Royal Hanoverian Guelphic Order, a Companion of the Bath, and a Knight of the Order of William of Holland.

Bibliography

BRETT-JAMES, ANTONY. *General Graham, Lord Lynedoch*. London, 1957.
— *The Hundred Days*. London, 1964.

CANNON, RICHARD. *The History of the 73rd Regiment*. London, 1855.

COSTELLO, EDWARD. *Adventures of a Soldier*. Ed. Antony Brett-James. London, 1967.

DALTON, CHARLES. *The Waterloo Roll Call*. 2nd edn. London, 1904.

FORTESCUE, J. W. *A History of the British Army*. London, 1910. Vols IX and X.

GODDARD and BOOTH. *Military Costumes of Europe*. London, 1812.

HARRIS. *Recollections of Rifleman Harris*. Ed. Henry Curling. London, 1848.

KELLY, C. *Battle of Waterloo*. London, 1835.

LOCKHART, J. G. *A History of Napoleon Bonaparte*. London, 1947.

NAYLOR, J. *Waterloo*. London, 1960.

ROPES, J. C. *The Campaign of Waterloo*. London, 1893.

WHEELER. *Letters of Private Wheeler, 1809–28*. Ed. Capt. B. H. Liddell Hart. London, 1952.

Index